1951

When Giants Played the Game

By Kerry Keene

SPORTS PUBLISHING L.L.C.
www.SportsPublishingLLC.com

ISBN: 1-58261-309-5

Director of Production: Susan M. Moyer
Dustjacket design: Christina Cary

SPORTS PUBLISHING L.L.C.
http://www.SportsPublishingLLC.com

Printed in the United States.

Contents

Acknowledgments

It is virtually impossible for one individual to complete a project such as this entirely on his or her own. I must start off by thanking Mike Pearson of Sports Publishing, who provided me with the idea that 1951 was a year in baseball that was well worth reliving.

As a member of the Society for American Baseball Research, I am greatly indebted to so many who have helped to further my own knowledge of the history of this great American phenomenon that is baseball. I have learned much as a member of this organization, and yet there is so much left to learn. I used to like to consider myself an historian, but now I realize that I am merely a student. Among my fellow members that I would like to thank specifically are Dick Thompson, Bill Deane, Stew Thornley, Paul Hirsh, Dick Johnson, Wayne McElreavy, David W. Smith, Christine Fry, and Gil Bogen.

I cannot forget my two friends Ray Sinibaldi and David Hickey, who remain so much a part of what I do. And I must give thanks to Zachary Keene, who helps to take much of the mystery out of this confounding machine known as the computer.

About the Author . . .

KERRY KEENE also authored *1960: The Last Pure Season* (2000) and co-authored *The Babe in Red Stockings* (1997) for Sports Publishing. A baseball historian, Keene is married, has two children, and resides in Raynham, Massachusetts.

Introduction

In the near 130 years of major league baseball, with countless home runs that have been hit, there are a half dozen or so that stand above as truly the most memorable. Babe Ruth's 60th in 1927; Roger Maris breaking that mark by one in 1961; Bill Mazeroski's Series winner in 1960; Hank Aaron eclipsing Babe in 1974; Carlton Fisk's dramatic 12th-inning game-ender in Game Six of the 1975 World Series; Joe Carter's Series winner of 1993.

A case for the home run slugged by New York Giants Bobby Thomson to win the National League playoffs of 1951 stands right amongst them in terms of sheer excitement and significance. Literally thousands of times over the years, the historic homer has been replayed, accompanied by the frantic voice of New York broadcaster Russ Hodges repeatedly shouting, "The Giants win the pennant! The Giants win the pennant!" With the game being broadcast live to U.S. military forces engaged in the Korean War, the classic home run earned its title as the "Shot heard 'round the world." Remarkably, a half-century later, Thomson and the Brooklyn pitcher who surrendered the home run, Ralph Branca, continue to make occasional appearances together and re-live their moment in the spotlight.

Though the events of October 3, 1951, remain a particularly prominent and noteworthy memory, so much more would occur in the baseball world at the threshold of the second half of the twentieth century. Both the National and American Leagues were celebrating milestones in '51— the National having been founded 75 years before, and the American now 50 years since its beginning as a major circuit in 1901. Both leagues seized the opportunities to honor their beginnings and the individuals who played a part.

Particularly noteworthy was the consistency that had reigned in the American League, retaining its eight-team format throughout its entire history. It had also not experienced a franchise shift since 1903, when the Baltimore team had relocated to New York.

Ah yes—New York. In his ambitious 18-hour 1994 documentary simply entitled "Baseball," filmmaker Ken Burns very fittingly titled Part Seven "The Capital of Baseball"—a reference to the city of New York in the decade of the 1950s, which thoroughly dominated the game during that era. It was there in 1951 that the career of an aging Joe DiMaggio intersected with that of a 19-year-old rookie Mickey Mantle for one shining, majestic season. As much as the baseball world marvelled at young Mantle's talent, they raved at the exploits of his rookie counterpart Willie Howard Mays.

Two young outfielders not yet 20 years old at the beginning of the 1951 season, poised to embark on major league careers that would see success beyond their wildest dreams.

The endings and beginnings of legendary careers in 1951 was not limited to New York centerfielders. The year would mark the first season in the 50-year history of the Philadelphia Athletics franchise that baseball's grand old man, Connie Mack, was not the team's manager, having finally stepped down late in 1950. At the same time, former longtime National League catcher Al Lopez was hired to take over the Cleveland Indians, beginning a managerial career that would result in him joining Mack in the Baseball Hall of Fame.

But one of the most unexpected endings of a baseball career occurred with the 1951 ouster of commissioner Albert "Happy" Chandler by a small group of team owners. Chandler had succeeded baseball's first commissioner, Judge Kenesaw Mountain Landis, in 1945, and had played a significant role in the integration of the major leagues—yet had now failed to receive sufficient support to have his contract renewed by the owners.

The search for Chandler's successor was a prominent sports story for many months in the first half of 1951 and would include such names as General Douglas MacArthur, future president Dwight Eisenhower, and FBI head J. Edgar Hoover. Though candidates were considered from many diverse areas, the powers that be ultimately turned to one of its own.

The summer of '51 also saw the return to baseball of maverick owner Bill Veeck, who had sold the Cleveland Indians two years prior. Veeck bought controlling interest in the St. Louis Browns and made news by bringing in a Negro League legend as well as one very noteworthy midget. As much as any man alive, Veeck saw baseball as entertainment.

So many historic events were to be documented on the sports pages during that storied year. The National Football League staged its first annual Pro Bowl in January, with Cleveland Browns legend Otto Graham starring at quarterback. Ben Hogan captured golf's 50th U.S. Open. College basketball experienced a devastating betting scandal involving four New York city universities in the same year as the death of "Shoeless" Joe Jackson. In the world of boxing, "Jersey" Joe Walcott defeated Ezzard Charles for the heavyweight championship, while Rocky Marciano worked his way up the rankings by beating an aging Joe Louis.

But it was baseball that clearly occupied the fondest place in the hearts of this country which numbered 155 million in 1951. It would be inconceivable at that time to hold a debate or to take a poll to determine which game would rightly be regarded as the "national pastime." It was that long-ago, black-and-white newsreel age when hallowed edifices such as Ebbets Field and the Polo Grounds were still thriving hosts to big-league ball; When Boston, Philadelphia, and St. Louis still had teams in both the A.L. and N.L.; and the Washington Senators existed if for no other reason than it was unfathomable that our nation's capital could be without a team; When no ballpark would be covered with a roof, and all ballplayers would tread upon real grass, continuing the long-standing practice of leaving their baseball mitts on that real grass of the playing field when it was their half of the inning to bat.

What baseball fan wouldn't get a kick out of turning back the clock 50 years to a time where the top price tickets in the major leagues was $3.00, and bleacher seats were commonly found for 50 cents—prices that had increased only minimally in more than two decades; when it was not uncommon for a game to take an even two hours to play from opening pitch to final out; when the vast majority of games were played in natural daylight; and where the minimum salary for a major leaguer was $5,000, with the average player making approximately $14,000? Rolling back five decades would also allow one to appreciate the broadcasting styles and signature lines of Brooklyn's Red Barber, the Yankees Mel Allen, Harry Caray, serving as voice of the Cardinals at that time, and so many others who have subsequently been honored for their work behind the microphone.

Baseball evokes nothing if not nostalgia for the longtime followers of the game. The Golden Anniversary of a golden season may just be the perfect time for reflection.

'51: ANNIVERSARIES OF THE LEAGUES

AS THE CALENDAR FLIPPED to nineteen hundred fifty-one and the second half of the twentieth century commenced, the United States all too soon found itself embroiled in another military conflict overseas less than six years removed from the conclusion of World War II. U. S. forces led by General Douglas MacArthur were joined by United Nations allies in an attempt to halt the spread of communism in South Korea. On the home front, the baby boom was in full swing, as was the television boom. Rapidly increasing numbers of households added RCA, Magnavox, and Philco sets and were tuning into shows such as "Star Theatre," "The Milton Berle Show," and "Ted Mack's Amateur Hour." The enduring favorite "I Love Lucy" would make its debut in October of that year.

For those who ventured outside the home for entertainment, driving to the local movie houses in Buick Roadmasters, Chevy Skylarks, and DeSotos, "The Greatest Show on Earth," "A Night at the Opera," "King Solomon's Mines," and "Branded" were but a few of their choices. Popular tunes filling the airwaves were "How high the moon" by Les Paul and Mary Ford, "Cry" by Johnnie Ray, "Sentimental Music" by Bing Crosby, and "Cold, cold heart" by Hank Williams.

Television and radio were increasingly becoming factors to the owners, players, and fans throughout the landscape of baseball. Heading into 1951, baseball commissioner Albert "Happy" Chandler signed a six-year, six million dollar deal with Gillette and the Mutual Broadcasting System for the rights to televise the World Series and All-Star games. Chandler stated that the money would mainly be applied to the players pension fund. In February of '51, the Brooklyn Dodgers signed a ten-year, 4.5 million dollar deal to have their games broadcast over WOR-TV and WMGM radio. At the same time, WPIX in New York purchased the rights to televise Yankees home games through 1956, and though the sum was undisclosed, a station official described it as "huge."

Many teams' broadcasters were becoming celebrities in their own rights —highly identifiable members of their organizations. Red Barber with the Dodgers; Mel Allen of the Yankees; Harry Caray with the Cardinals; Ernie Harwell in his pre-Tiger days along with Russ Hodges of the Giants; and a young Curt Gowdy, beginning the first year in '51 of a 16-year stay with the Red Sox that helped to launch an extremely successful broadcast career. So many men behind the microphones at this time would go on to be recognized for their outstanding work by the Baseball Hall of Fame.

Milestones were being set in the area of television baseball broadcasting with several teams in 1951. The Washington Senators televised a road game for the first time on April 27 back in D.C. with Arch McDonald and Bob Wolff calling the action from Yankee Stadium. The Braves-Dodgers game on August 11 was the first major league game ever televised in color.

Baseball was clearly gaining increased exposure in the electronic media, and National League president Ford Frick in particular greatly supported the use of television and radio as promotional tools for the sport. The Boston Braves had even begun sponsoring a weekly television show called "Baseball in your living room" that aired every Thursday evening in the Boston area. The Cleveland

Indians were televising all home games and were broadcasting all games home and away over radio. Management felt that as long as the team was winning, attendance would not be affected.

Many minor league officials however, were greatly concerned over major league games being broadcast in their areas. Paul Fagan for one, owner of the Pacific Coast League's San Francisco Seals complained loudly to major league officials that the meager crowds for his Seals, the Oakland Oaks, and other teams in the circuit were a direct result of big-league competition on the airwaves. The Mutual Broadcasting System was airing a "Game of the Day" over 545 radio stations coast to coast. Some were seeking measures to halt the broadcast, going so far as to suggest legislation. Even one major league owner, Fred Saigh of the St. Louis Cardinals, was not happy with the television situation. His chief complaint was that television money garnered by some teams was upsetting the balance of power in the major leagues. Bemoaning the lack of competitive balance is apparently not a concept that was created in the late 1990s. In an editorial in its May 23, 1951 issue, *The Sporting News* questioned the notion, calling for measures to be taken to prevent rich teams from dominating poorer teams. A week later in the May 30 issue, Detroit baseball writer Ray Gillespie wrote:

> "It's only May 24, yet the race is over for the Philadelphia Athletics and the St. Louis Browns, which are 13 and 15 games behind. Wouldn't it be charitable to let 'em go duck hunting and trout fishing now instead of making 'em stay on for their nuisance value?"

In a more potentially threatening action against baseball, new challenges to its Reserve Clause surfaced in the Spring of '51—two full decades before Curt Flood made his attempt. The age-old practice of a team being able to retain the right to players after their contract expired was coming under fire.

Former minor league pitcher Jim Prendergast filed suit in Federal court in Utica, New York, in April, to challenge the Reserve Clause, as did another pitcher, former Yankee minor leaguer George Earl Toolson, who filed in L. A. Federal court in early May. Yet another minor leaguer, Walter Kowalski, filed a similar suit in Cincinnati in June. Emanuel Celler, Chairman of the Special Sub-committee on Monopolies created by the House Judiciary Committee announced in May that hearings on baseball's status with respect to any need for federal regulation would start during the summer. At that time, the legality of the Reserve Clause was to be examined closely. Congressman Celler (D-N.Y.) insisted that if it was found to be detrimental to any of the parties involved, it must be abolished. He added, however, that the sole aim was the protection of baseball.

Jack Corbett, owner of the minor league El Paso team filed suit in U.S. District Court in Cincinnati in April. He had been forbidden by Organized baseball to sign Mexican League players due to an agreement made by commissioner Chandler. Corbett maintained that this constituted an attempt to monopolize trade among foreign countries and was in violation of Sherman antitrust laws.

Player representatives of each league, Ralph Kiner of the N.L. and Tiger pitcher Fred Hutchinson were in favor of the Reserve Clause. Said Hutchinson, "As a player representative of the American League, I have never heard any complaints against it." Kiner added, "I don't see how baseball could operate without a reserve clause. It's as much a part of the game as the rules we use on the field."

Senator Edward Johnson of Colorado, who also happened to be the president of the Western League urged baseball to obtain legislation that would affirm and confirm the legality of the clause in order to avert upcoming legal action. Johnson expressed a desire to assist, but asked for the wholehearted support of Organized baseball. Dodgers owner Walter O'Malley took exception to the challenges against baseball's business, and at a luncheon in New York City at the end of May he called for baseball's friends to stand up and be counted, and stated:

"We [major league owners and officials] are being pictured in Washington as mobsters, enslaving ballplayers. I'm sure there are things more important for our top-ranking legislators to be concerned with at this time. I'd like to see someone come out in defense of baseball for a change; not to mention the good it does.

"I haven't heard any genuine ballplayer, whose record and his bat speak for him, complain of his 'serfdom' or of his being enslaved."

While the Korean War did not have the same drastic effect on Major League Baseball as World War II had the decade before, its impact was felt by the game in many ways.

Although no major superstars would be called to serve in the military in 1951 as they were between 1942 and '45, several younger players were putting their careers on hold upon notifications from draft boards. Among the more noteworthy were: Curt Simmons (left-handed pitcher, Phillies), Whitey Ford (left-handed pitcher, Yankees), Art Houtteman (right-handed pitcher, Tigers), Del Crandall (catcher, Braves), Jim Lemon (outfielder, Washington), Johnny Antonelli (LHP, Braves), Preston Ward (first baseman, Cubs), and Billy Loes (RHP, Dodgers).

The drafting of so many younger players into the military had an effect on the scouting philosophies of many major league teams. Many were now turning toward established minor-leaguers in their late 20s due to their unlikelihood of being called for duty, as well as putting more of a premium on Latin and Cuban ballplayers, whose countries were not involved in the conflict. It seems as though an international military situation may well have had an impact on furthering the increase in baseball's talent pool beyond the U.S. border.

Those who would be playing in 1951 could expect to do so without any significant raise in salary over the previous year. The United States Wage Stabilization Board ruled on April 2 that base-ball was subject to regulations imposed on other industries and that no player could be paid more than his team's highest paid player had been paid in 1950. Up until the ruling though, there had been very few players holding out for more money, as most realized there would be very little sympathy from the public toward them in war-time. Players were generally just happy not being called into the

military and were concerned that holding out could only bring un-
wanted attention to themselves.

Throughout major league Spring Training camps, workouts
were being operated in a much more serious, even militaristic style,
in light of American men and women serving in Korea. There was
much less golfing and swimming in off hours, and little of the high
jinks and clowning around usually found at training camps. Al
Schacht, known for many years for his baseball comedy routines
visited and entertained troops in Korea. He reported back that the
soldiers loved to talk and read about what was going on in baseball,
and they begged for issues of *The Sporting News*. An effort was
subsequently made to ship many copies overseas.

The Sporting News, at 20 cents per issue in 1951, had been
covering baseball like few other publications since its debut in 1886.
Many fans throughout the country took the time to peruse "the
bible of baseball" as it was known with its extensive coverage of the
game during their periodic trips to the local barber shop. Through
an arrangement with the makers of Kreml Hair Tonic in 1951,
35,000 shops throughout the United States received a weekly issue
for customers, as they realized that one of the chief topics of discussion amongst them was baseball.

The two major league circuits would be celebrating significant anniversary milestones during 1951—the National League having been formed 75 years earlier, and the American League recog-
nizing 50 years since its debut. The N.L. chose the exact site of its
official founding on February 2, 1876, to hold its three-day "Diamond Jubilee" celebration. Originally built in 1868, the eight-story
Grand Central Hotel located at Broadway and Third St. was the
Waldorf of its time back in 1876 when a group of magnates assembled to form the new circuit. Three quarters of a century to the
day later in 1951, the hotel now known as the Broadway Central
would be the site of a three-day affair to honor the N.L.'s beginnings as well as its entire history. Fifteen living Hall of Famers were
on hand for the occasion, including Cy Young, Ty Cobb, Rogers
Hornsby, George Sisler, Tris Speaker, and others. The affair included the unveiling of a bronze plaque on the exterior of the Broad-

way Central, formally unveiled by New York Mayor Vincent Impelliter, as Mel Allen acted as emcee. N.L. president Frick made a brief speech and introduced all of the Hall of Famers present. *The Sporting News* in its February 14 issue editorialized: "In the long history of professional baseball, the game has never seen anything quite like the diamond jubilee celebration of the National League in New York starting on February 2, and running through the next two days and nights."

It also added: "The success of the National League's jubilee once again drives home a point which *The Sporting News* has been making for many years—that the fans and the writers are vastly interested in the past, as well as the present and the future."

Virtually every major league team had planned to observe their particular circuit's anniversary in their own manner, many holding Old-Timer's Days to take place at various times throughout the season.

Also at this time, both the National and American Leagues unveiled commemorative patches that would be worn on every team's uniforms throughout the 1951 season. The N.L.'s was a simple logo depicting a baseball glove and a ball, while the A.L.'s, slightly more elaborate, was a shield with crossed bats and a ball with the words "American League 1901 GOLDEN ANNIVERSARY." Also part of the A.L.'s anniversary observation was that an All-Star team of the first 50 years would be named, with Connie Mack heading a committee made up mainly of writers.

Two other significant anniversaries were being observed as well by the baseball world in 1951. The National Association, which was the governing body of the entire minor league branch of Organized baseball was, like the A.L., now 50 years old. And the Spalding baseball was celebrating its 75th anniversary as the official ball of the National League. Albert Goodwill Spalding, elected to the Hall of Fame for his pioneering feats as a pitcher in the 1860s and 1870s as well as being a co-founder of the N.L. in 1876, convinced his fellow magnates to use the ball that his sporting goods firm was manufacturing. It would be the only brand of baseball that the National League would use until it switched to Rawlings in the 1970s.

American League

National League

The anniversary logos worn on the sleeve of major league uniforms to commemorate the American League's 50th and the National League's 75th anniversary in 1951.

As major league Spring Training camps opened in late February of '51, there was no shortage of high expectations, developing situations, and serious question marks. The two-time defending World Champion New York Yankees found themselves surrounded by different scenery this spring, having swapped training sites with the New York Giants.

The Yanks would be preparing to defend their crown in Phoenix, Arizona, while Leo Durocher's Giants took over the St. Petersburg Florida site. The switch was prompted by Yankees co-owner

Del Webb, who resided in Phoenix and had wanted to bring his team to the Southwestern city for some time. Yankee players observed in short order that with this being cattle country, great cuts of beef were plentiful, as opposed to St. Petersburg, where seafood was the primary choice. Webb had purchased $50 cowboy hats for each player to wear around Phoenix. New York baseball writer Dan Daniel wrote of Yogi Berra: "Hopalong Berra looks especially funny, as his hat happens to be too small for him."

Berra also complained that it was difficult to find a good selection of comic books in Phoenix. Because of his slightly odd, somewhat unathletic appearance, as well as his penchant for noteworthy quotes, Yogi was often the recipient of good-natured teasing from the press. In March of '51, Berra said of the writers, "Sometimes it is tough to tell what these guys write about me. My wife, she don't like stories which make me out to be a dope." Former great Yankee catcher Bill Dickey, who had tutored Berra in the fine points behind the plate, said at this time that his student was greatly underrated simply because his appearance was working against him.

Berra signed a contract in the Spring of '51 calling for him to make $30,000 that season, surpassing Dickey's $28,000 as the highest paid catcher in Yankee history. Of his contract amount, Berra revealed a slightly different side, saying, "I got responsibilities. I got to support my mom and dad. I have a wife and a son. I have to dress like a Yankee, live like a Yankee, act like a Yankee. That takes dough." When it came to "acting like a Yankee," Berra said his roommate Phil Rizzuto taught him many things, such as how to act in hotel dining rooms, how to handle the press and the fans, how to conduct himself socially. He even convinced Yogi—though apparently not with complete success—to stop reading comic books and start reading novels and detective stories.

Indeed, this was a time when it was truly special to be a Yankee; a mystique seemed to permeate throughout the organization. Beat writer Dan Daniel pointed out in a column in May that even Yankee minor-leaguers were expected to "dress like Yankees" and

YOGI BERRA. *Detroit Tigers pitcher Dizzy Trout said of him in 1951:"We pitch to him with psychology, but Yogi doesn't know what psychology is. But give him a bat and Yogi smartens up."*

carry themselves accordingly. The team had acquired pitcher Bob Muncrief before the beginning of the '51 season, and though he had been on two American League pennant winners—the '44 Browns and the '48 Indians—he said the biggest thrill of his 18-year pro career was putting on a Yankee uniform for the first time. He said, "I walked over in front of the mirror and stood there for five minutes looking at the words 'New York' on the front of my shirt."

But it was the player who may have best exemplified what it was to be a Yankee, Joe DiMaggio, who was among the biggest topics of speculation in the Yankee camp. Would the 1951 season be the final one of his legendary playing career? The emergence in training camp of a 19-year-old Mickey Mantle, being converted from a shortstop to the outfield as a possible successor to Joe D. fueled speculation. An article on Mantle in the March 28, 1951 *Sporting News* by Daniel was entitled, "Two-Way Slugger fitted for Clipper's Shoes." Though Joe was sending out signals that this would indeed be his swan song, many in the organization felt he would return in 1952.

A big part of the Yankee attack would continue to be Rizzuto—leader of the infield and number-two hitter. "Scooter" was coming off a 1950 season for which he won the American League Most Valuable Player Award, the *Sport Magazine* Athlete of the Year Award, the Ray Hickok Athlete of the Year Belt; was named *The Sporting News* Player of the Year, and was given the Sid Mercer Award by the New York Baseball Writers as the Player of the Year. Rizzuto had been given a rather significant $15,000 raise going into '51, increasing his salary to $50,000 for the season. Despite a paycheck that was considered princely for the times, Phil still maintained his off-season job with the Washington Shop menswear store in New York.

The pitching staff of the defending World Champions was led by two 21-game winners, left-hander Eddie Lopat and righty Vic Raschi, along with 17-game winner Allie Reynolds. Berra said of Lopat at the beginning of the season, "He has about as fine a collection of pitches as anybody in the business today, in the A.L.

PHIL RIZZUTO. *When he was mentioned in trade rumors after the '51 season, it was said that fans would tear down Yankee Stadium if he were dealt. Phil was extremely attached to his four-year-old baseball mitt and said that season, "I wouldn't part with my glove for anything in the world."*

anyway. He throws hard, he throws slow. He has a fine curve. He pitches a good knuckler, and maybe he should work on it more than he does. He has a screwball, and a slider, and a great curve."

Reynolds, despite an ailing elbow that severely limited his Spring Training activities, was destined for extremely noteworthy performances in 1951. The staff would be without young Whitey Ford, however, who won nine straight games in 1950 after being called up from Kansas City and who was also the winner in the Series-clinching Game Four of the World Series versus Philadelphia. The lefty would be spending the season in the military, pitching for the Fort Monmouth (N.J.) team. Young second baseman Billy Martin, who like Ford had debuted with the Yankees in 1950, was also serving in the military at this time. Another young second baseman, Gil McDougald, who was the MVP of the Texas League in 1950 with Beaumont, was poised to make a big splash and add a big award to his trophy case. The status of third baseman Bobby Brown was uncertain going into the season. He was in an unusual circumstance for a ballplayer, having graduated medical school and serving an internship at the time in San Francisco.

The Yankees were the highest paid team in baseball in 1951 with a payroll of roughly $500,000, and despite a few question marks, Stengel said in mid-March that the team's owners would get their money's worth with a third straight pennant. Few managers in history found themselves in a more favorable situation than Stengel had when he took over the Yankees. Prior to his first season with the team in 1949, he had managed in the National League for nine seasons, heading both the Braves and the Dodgers. In those nine campaigns, Stengel's teams finished above .500 only once (by two games), and never placed higher than fifth in the league.

The team expected to be the major stumbling block in New York's pursuit of yet another pennant was the Boston Red Sox. Owner Tom Yawkey had spent money so lavishly in an attempt to bring a championship to Boston that many writers referred to them as the "Gold Sox" or the "Millionaires." Ted Williams had signed in February to play for $100,000, though some later said the figure could actually be as high as $125,000. General Manager Joe Cronin

GEORGE KELL. *George Kell of the Detroit Tigers was regarded as baseball's premier all-around third baseman by 1951.*

had made deals in the off-season to acquire pitchers Ray Scarborough and Bill Wight, along with longtime Indians shortstop Lou Boudreau, and many felt that Boston was now the favorite. When Tigers manager Red Rolfe heard about Boston acquiring the two pitchers, he snapped "That does it, if they don't win the pennant this time, they ought to give it up."

On joining the Red Sox, Scarborough said, "I'll tell you one thing that's nice. Life ought to be a lot easier now that I don't have to pitch to Ted Williams, Junior Stephens, Bobby Doerr, Billy Goodman, and Johnny Pesky. Nice to have them *for* me instead of against me." Boudreau, who had been released by Cleveland after the '50 season also had offers from the Yankees and the Senators. He accepted the $40,000 offer from Boston, $10,000 less than Washington's offer because he liked their pennant chances better, plus the possibility of getting the managerial job eventually. A good indication of the Red Sox batting power was that 1950 A.L. batting champion Billy Goodman would be batting seventh in the order. Bobby Doerr expressed confidence in the team's chances, saying, "I know we've been winning it on paper the past several seasons, but this year we can do it ON the field."

Yet there always seemed to be some obstacle that prevented the Red Sox ship from sailing smoothly. Ted Williams himself told a radio interviewer in mid-March, "There's always dissension on this club. Has been ever since I came to it. Somebody's always fighting with the manager or among one another." New York writer Dan Daniel acknowledged Boston's powerful lineup and opined that nobody could beat them but themselves, but was also quick to point out their long history of frustration. Steve O'Leary of the *Boston American* wrote of his personal frustration in his column:

> "Each October you swear you'll never do it again, but when the Springtime rolls around you get that same old feeling that the Red Sox can't miss this time. So you pick 'em to win and wait for the roof to fall in next September."
>
> *The Sporting News*—April 4, 1951

TED WILLIAMS. *Ted Williams, shown here on his first day at Spring Training of 1951 in Sarasota, Florida. Ted was working hard to return from a broken elbow that caused him to miss half of the 1950 season.*

Ignoring his better judgment, O'Leary went on record in the April 18 issue on Boston's pennant chances: "Seemingly no excuse to miss this time and Steve O'Neill should lead them to the pennant in his first full season."

Writer Tom Meany, noted author of the first major biography of Babe Ruth in 1948 wrote an article in *Collier's Magazine* in which he blamed much of the Red Sox troubles on the Boston baseball writers. Entitled "Baseball's hottest seat," he referred to the Boston press as "an anchor around the neck of the Red Sox." A half-century later, some may still feel there is a bit of truth in this statement.

The Cleveland Indians, who could claim Bob Hope as part owner, were beginning a new era of leadership with rookie manager Al Lopez. Popular outfielder Larry Doby, named Cleveland baseball's "Man of the Year" for 1950 said at an off-season banquet that he had heard good reports on Lopez and that he hoped he was "as lucky as Stengel."

Any team with a pitching staff like Cleveland possessed had to be considered a contender, as most felt that the rotation of Bob Lemon, Bob Feller, Mike Garcia, and Early Wynn was the top mound corps in the league. Lemon had earned his place as the highest paid pitcher in baseball, and Feller appeared to be in his best form since 1946 when he struck out 348 batters. The everyday lineup featured big first baseman Luke Easter, considered indispensable to the offensive attack, and saw the emergence of Cuban Orestes "Minnie" Minoso, poised to see his first full season of major league action at 28 years old. In the Spring of '51, Minoso was given a stellar endorsement from none other than Satchel Paige, who said, "They're going to have a lot of trouble with him . . . he's the fastest fellow I've ever seen. He's lightning."

The Detroit Tigers were led by the A.L.'s premier lefty, Hal Newhouser, who would be turning 30 years old in May, yet was already closing in on his 200th career victory.

Their most noteworthy star in the lineup was perennial all-star third baseman George Kell. Using the smallest bat in the major leagues at the time, Kell was thought by Ted Williams to be the most dangerous hitter active in baseball. "Kell just keeps going,

BOB LEMON. *The Indians ace, who was said to be baseball's highest-paid pitcher in 1951, came into the season with three straight 20-win seasons.*

hitting steadily all the time," Williams said, shortly after the season began. "Some other hitters may get more publicity because of their batting feats, but Kell's a real good hitter who is always up there right near the top."

The team occupying the South side of Chicago, the White Sox, had 42-year-old former catcher Paul Richards as their new skipper for 1951. Early in the season, Richards hailed his 23-year-old Venezuelan shortstop Chico Carrasquel as "the standout player in our lineup." Carrasquel was receiving accolades from many around the game as the best defensive shortstop in baseball. Phil Rizzuto said at this time: "Chico's the best in either league without question. He can do everything in the field."

Lou Boudreau added of Chico: "Best young shortstop I've ever seen come up in our league since Rizzuto in 1941." He was hugely popular in his native Venezuela, and many of the country's citizens adopted the White Sox as the team they followed because of him. Each day during the season, its newspapers carried updates of Chico and the White Sox' performances on Page One.

CHICO CARRASQUEL. *In only his second season, Carrasquel was already being hailed in 1951 as the best defensive shortstop in the game. He set a major league record that season, going 53 games without an error.*

Carrasquel was teamed with double-play partner Nellie Fox, who was called the "toy terrier." Fox previously had difficulty turning the double play, but was coached in the art in Spring Training of '51 by the recently retired Cleveland second baseman Joe Gordon.

The improvement Fox showed at "turning two" that season was dramatic, and he and Carrasquel would make a stellar double play combination for years to come.

NELLIE FOX. *When he had played with a badly bruised foot for several days in 1951, White Sox trainer Mush Esler said, "I've handled a lot of rugged football players, but this little guy has the biggest heart I've ever seen. Nobody else could have walked on that foot."*

As the Philadelphia Athletics Spring Training camp opened in West Palm Beach, Florida in late February, it would be doing so without Connie Mack at the helm for the first time in the team's 50-year history. The reigns were handed over to coach Jimmie Dykes, who inherited a team that had the majors' worst record in 1950 with 102 losses.

Mack, often referred to as "baseball's oldest inhabitant" was a daily visitor at the Athletics camp. Still serving as the team's president, he was frequently seen surrounded by fans seeking autographs, and the 88-year-old patriarch of the Philadelphia team was ever accommodating. He reminisced with reporters about memorable past Spring Training camps, and said that this was the 64th he had

CONNIE MACK. *Baseball's 'grand old man' Connie Mack, shown here with Bill Veeck.*

attended, the first being as a catcher with the National League's Washington Capitals back in 1888 held in Jacksonville, Florida.

The St. Louis Browns were unquestionably the least stable of all American League franchises, seemingly on the verge of bankruptcy. The team only drew a total of 247,000 fans to Sportsman's Park in 1950, and management claimed it would need to draw 500,000 in '51 to make ends meet. In March of '51, Browns owners Charley and Bill DeWitt were forced to borrow $600,000 from a St. Louis bank to cover their debts. Fred Miller, owner of Miller Brewing Company in Milwaukee was said to be very interested in buying the Browns and moving them to that city. Milwaukee had begun construction on what would become County Stadium, and expected it to be ready for play in the Spring of 1952. Some were suggesting that the Browns move to Los Angeles, and it was recalled that such a move very nearly occurred ten years prior. Don Barnes, the Browns owner at that time was set to announce the move in early December of 1941, when the attack on Pearl Harbor put everything on hold. But by mid-summer of 1951, a new ownership situation would come around that, while it didn't improve the team's place in the standings, certainly added a dash of color and carnival atmosphere.

Over in the National League, the Philadelphia Phillies were about to defend their 1950 league championship, though not many prognosticators gave them much of a chance of doing so successfully. The prevailing thought was that they wouldn't sneak up on anyone this season, and the loss of young lefty Curt Simmons to the military was a blow to the pitching staff. Many also questioned if reliever Jim Konstanty could duplicate the form that saw him capture the league MVP Award by winning 16 games in relief. The Phils did still feature exciting performers in Granny Hamner, Richie Ashburn, Del Ennis, and Robin Roberts. Hamner was in all likelihood the best defensive shortstop in the N.L., and Ashburn, emerging as a star performer was an excellent center fielder who may have been the fastest in the league going from home to first. In its "Hats Off" column in the June 20 issue of *The Sporting News*, the following was written of Ashburn:

"Some men are born to greatness, some achieve it by fine spirit, hard work, and a burning determination. Richie Ashburn, brilliant center fielder of the Phillies, gained stardom by the latter route. Handicapped by a comparatively weak arm, not blessed with the stature or power of some other outfielders, Ashburn has one tremendous gift—speed—and he has parlayed this talent with courage and grit to become one of the finest outfielders in baseball."

Ennis, a slugging right fielder who swung a 44-ounce bat and was coming off a 1950 season that would be the most productive of his career. Twenty-four-year-old right hander Robin Roberts recorded the first of his six straight 20-win seasons.

The Brooklyn Dodgers, whom the Phillies had eliminated from pennant contention on the final day of the 1950 season were being taken over on the field by Chuck Dressen. After reportedly being turned down for the managerial position by former Giants star first baseman Bill Terry, Dodgers owner O'Malley turned to Dressen, manager of the Pacific Coast League's Oakland Oaks. Off the field, the Dodgers were no longer being directed by highly accomplished executive Branch Rickey, who left the team in the offseason to take over as general manager of the Pittsburgh Pirates. Upon his departure, center fielder Duke Snider commented: "A lot of us feel more secure now that Rickey's gone. We're not afraid of being sold now . . . if he could get that dollar for you, he'd sell you."

Snider was emerging as a top performer in the N.L., and some observers felt he could be the next Stan Musial. O'Malley was of the opinion that he was already the best player in the league, but others might have argued that the distinction would belong to Snider's teammate Jackie Robinson. Robinson turned 32 years old at the beginning of 1951, but was still performing like a player in his prime. Looking ahead to the '51 season, he expressed the desire to run more under Dressen. "That's the kind of game I like to play," Robinson said in January. Jackie had taken Dressen's suggestion of trying the Mayo Clinic diet over the winter, which consisted largely of grapefruit and eggs, and had shed several pounds as a result.

J. Roy Stockton, *St. Louis Post-Dispatch* sports editor wrote of the Dodgers at the start of the season: "Best team in the league, position for position, with perhaps the best bench to boot." The best team also carried the highest payroll in the N.L. at nearly $500,000, and expectations naturally ran high. Burt Shotton, who had managed the Dodgers from 1947 to '50 said from his home in Florida before '51 Spring Training began that the New York Giants were the only team with a chance to beat Brooklyn this season. Dodgers vice-president Buzzie Bavasi added: "We feel that we are the club to beat, and the Giants are the boys who will prove the most troublesome."

The Giants had finished the 1950 season on a good note, winning 50 of the last 72 games. They were entering their fourth season with Leo Durocher at the helm after he had managed the Dodgers for nine seasons. This only added to a Giants-Dodgers rivalry that at the time was as intense a rivalry as there had been in baseball history. New York could counter with a capable starting pitching staff that included Sal Maglie, Jim Hearn, and Larry Jansen. Their lineup contained productive hitters Hank Thompson and Bobby Thomson, as well as Monte Irvin, who was on the verge of his breakout season. The double-play combination was among the league's better, with shortstop Alvin Dark and second baseman Eddie Stanky. Both were intelligent ballplayers with leadership qualities that took them on to major league managerial careers. Just before Spring Training of '51, Stanky said of Durocher "All (he) asks is that you hustle all the time. I've seen him bawl out .320 hitters for loafing, but he'll stick with a .230 guy and never say a word providing he hustles." Jack Orr of the *New York Compass* presented another side of Leo when he wrote in June: "To know him is to get stabbing, aching sensations in various places."

The man who had been Durocher's boss years earlier. Branch Rickey, admitted in early '51 that he had taken on a monumental challenge in attempting to rebuild the Pirates, and said they were " . . . far outmatched in manpower by the Dodgers and Cardinals." "The Pirates are the weakest team with which I have ever been associated."

Rickey doubled the number of scouts for the organization and also began actively seeking out more Negro ballplayers. He made the assessment that the only Pirate players currently of first division stature were Ralph Kiner and Wally Westlake.

Kiner had now led the N.L. in home runs for an unprecedented fifth straight season, and his slugging had given a tremendous boost to the Pirates attendance in recent years.

He showed off his phenomenal power in the Spring of '51 when he launched a 500-foot home run in early April in an exhibition game versus the Phillies at New Orleans. One of the higher paid players in the game at $65,000 per year, Kiner's popularity allowed him to branch out to many high-profile endeavors outside the game. After the 1950 season, he opened up an office in Pittsburgh to house Ralph Kiner Enterprises Inc., which handled endorsements, personal appearances, and such. He had appeared on a few television shows in Hollywood over the winter, including "Truth or Consequences", and was to begin his own show that would air in Pittsburgh on Saturday nights beginning in April. "Ralph Kiner's" Restaurant opened up on Diamond Street in Pittsburgh in the summer of '51, and he also operated a sporting goods store in Alhambra, California. The 28-year-old Kiner was even hailed for his sartorial sense as the Custom Tailors Guild of America named him one of the best-dressed men in the country in March. To top it off, Ralph landed a big prize when in June, he announced his engagement to the National Indoor Women's Tennis champion, Nancy Chaffee. The announcement came at a private party held at a fancy restaurant about an hour after Kiner hit a home run to win a game. The next day, Miss Chaffee, sporting a two-carat diamond ring, flew to England to play Wimbledon. The headline in that day's *New York Daily News* was "Kiner wins game—and girl!"

Another National Leaguer who was extremely popular with fans and still in the midst of his prime productive years was Cardinal favorite Stan Musial. New St. Louis player-manager Marty Marion couldn't have asked for a more likeable, agreeable player to build his team around as he began his managerial career. Musial would spend most of his career bouncing between left field, right

TED WILLIAMS AND RALPH KINER. *Two of baseball's premier sluggers take a moment to chat before the All-Star Game.*

field, and first base, but said at the beginning of Spring Training: "I'll play wherever I can help the club most. I prefer the outfield, especially right field, but if Marty thinks I'll serve him best at first base, that's where I'll play." The highest paid player in the history of the National League at $75,000, Musial was occasionally criti-

STAN MUSIAL. *Stan the Man received more All-Star votes in 1951 than any other player in baseball.*

cized for lacking color. Sportswriter Tom Meany responded to the criticism " . . . if colorless means paying strict attention to business, staying in shape and being obliging and courteous, then the adjective fits Musial."

The pennant races, particularly in the National League were certainly to be colorful affairs in 1951. The Sporting News had polled 204 members of the Baseball Writers Association of America in early April regarding their pennant predictions. The Red Sox were the overwhelming favorite in the A.L. garnering 149 votes, with the Yankees a distant second with only 32. J. Roy Stockton wrote of the Red Sox: "Outstanding power, backed by impressive pitching staff . . . should be in front by 10 or 15 games on October 1." The esteemed J.G. Taylor Spink wrote: "The Yankees are not going to win again because their older players are showing the signs of wear, their pitching in general is uncertain, and their relief hurling in particular is most unimpressive."

The so-called experts viewed the N.L. race as being a bit closer, with New York neighbors the Giants and Dodgers likely occupying the top two spots. Ninety-nine voters had Durocher's Giants capturing the flag, with 69 favoring Brooklyn's 'Bums'. Only 24 of the 204 gave the Phillies a chance of returning to the Series. Even Phils manager Eddie Sawyer, admitting how badly they would miss lefty Curt Simmons predicted that the Dodgers would prevail. Dodgers owner Walter O'Malley came as close as anyone when he said early in the season that the N.L. race is going to be awfully tough on anyone with ulcers.

It would have been nearly impossible to imagine just how accurate O'Malley's prediction would be.

2

RAISING THE CURTAIN ON THE '51 CAMPAIGN

IN THE DAYS PRIOR TO THE OFFICIAL OPENING of the 1951 championship season, ten of the 16 big-league teams engaged in the time-honored tradition of competing in exhibition series against their crosstown rivals from the other major league. In an age when most teams still traveled by train, participating in the inter-city series meant taking a brief bus ride at most, or in the case of St. Louis and Philadelphia, merely being declared the visiting team in their home park.

The Boston Red Sox earned bragging rights in their city by sweeping their N.L. counterparts, the Braves, on April 13, 14, and 15; the first two at Braves Field and the final a mile away at Fenway Park. The Philadelphia Athletics and Phillies, who shared Shibe Park as their home field, squared off at the same time, with the N.L. champ Phils taking two of three. The Yankees and Dodgers engaged in a three-game set on those same three days as well, the first at Yankee Stadium and the final two at Ebbets Field. Brooklyn won

Games One and Three, but what was most worth remembering was that 19-year-old Mickey Mantle was making his first appearance of any kind in a game in New York City on April 14 at Ebbets. The next day, the rookie gave a sign of things to come by smacking a home run and three singles.

Rounding out the City Series' were the two Midwestern affairs in St. Louis and Chicago, consisting of two games each. The Cardinals and Browns, who shared Sportsman's Park split their series, while the Cubs took both from the South Side White Sox, one in each team's park.

It was a week when General Douglas MacArthur was making news by being relieved of command of forces in Korea by President Truman. Eight days later, the general made his memorable farewell speech before Congress in which he uttered the line "Old Soldiers never die.....they just fade away."

Opening Day at Yankee Stadium on Tuesday, April 17 was accompanied by much pomp and ceremony. Phil Rizzuto was presented with the Kenesaw Mountain Landis Award as the A.L. MVP for 1950; general manager George Weiss received *The Sporting News* Executive of the Year honor; and all Yankees from the '50 team were presented with their World Series rings. The 44,860 in attendance watched soldier Whitey Ford in his Army uniform throw out the first ball.

It was during the pregame activities that the Yankee Stadium crowd heard for the first time the voice of public address announcer Bob Sheppard, who was still behind the microphone five decades later. On May 7, 2000, Sheppard was honored for his work with a plaque at the Stadium's fabled Monument Park. Two months later, on July 23 at the annual Baseball Hall of Fame induction ceremony, Sheppard donated to the Hall the microphone that he had used in his first game back in 1951.

The game itself marked the official beginning of young Mantle's major league career, and the first time both he and Joe DiMaggio appeared in the Yankee outfield together in a game that mattered. Mantle, batting third in the order and playing right field stroked an RBI single as the Yankees, behind Vic Raschi shut out the rival Red Sox 5-0. The team was honored that evening at the Hotel Concourse Plaza by the People of the Bronx civic organization.

PRESIDENT HARRY TRUMAN. *President Harry Truman, tossing out the first ball at the Opening Game between Washington and Philadelphia.*

That same evening, the Philadelphia Athletics staged what would be the first night game opener in American League history as they hosted the Washington Senators.

Connie Mack sat in the stands for the first time ever for a season's opener, and in a pre-game ceremony was presented with a bronze bust in his likeness. Jimmie Dykes' debut as manager of the Athletics was spoiled by the Senators with a 6-1 loss.

As was tradition, the Cincinnati Reds, recognized as baseball's first all-professional team back in 1869, kicked off the major league season hosting the Pittsburgh Pirates on April 16. In honor of the N.L.'s 75th anniversary, pre-game ceremonies featured 88-year-old former Reds outfielder Dummy Hoy dressed in a circa 1876 uniform. Hoy, a deaf mute, had roamed the outfield for Cincinnati from 1894 through 1897. The game went on despite freezing temperatures and snow flurries, but one of the more noteworthy aspects was Ralph Kiner's playing first base for the first time in his spectacular career rather than his customary left field. Detroit fans, who braved temperatures that dipped to 37 degrees on April 17 witnessed the opener versus Cleveland that turned out to be quite a pitchers duel. Bob Lemon hurled a two-hit 2-1 win for the Indians to top Hal Newhouser's complete game eight-hitter. Larry Doby scored the winning run in the ninth inning on shortstop Johnny Lipon's fumble of Jim Hegan's grounder.

Two other openers took place over in the National League that same afternoon. At Ebbets Field in Brooklyn, Jackie Robinson's two-run homer in the sixth was all the Dodgers could muster against Robin Roberts as the N.L champion Phillies prevailed 5-2.

In Boston, the Braves drew only 6,081 spectators who had little to cheer about as New York Giants right hander Larry Jansen allowed just five hits in the 4-0 shutout. The following day, only 2,700 came out to Braves Field to see the two teams play.

Three days later on April 20, the Giants would host their own opener at New York's ancient and cavernous Polo Grounds. The visiting archrival Dodgers spoiled the day with Don Newcombe tossing a complete game five-hitter as Brooklyn won 7-3. To add insult to injury, the Dodgers snagged the next two games in heartbreaking fashion for a series sweep. Game Two on the 21st saw Brooklyn score five unanswered runs in the last three innings to win 7-3. In the series finale the following day, Carl Furillo hit a tenth-inning home run off Sal Maglie to win. Maglie had struck out Furillo earlier in the game and Giants manager Leo Durocher, who managed Carl with the Dodgers insisted he couldn't hit a sidearm pitch from a right hander, which he did. The Giants, who were favored to win by so many were now on their way to losing 11 straight games.

The Washington Senators home opener had been set to occur on April 16, however rain forced its postponement. President Truman had been issued his Gold Season Pass from Senators owner Clark Griffith in early April, but had to be phoned at the White House this Monday and informed that the festivities would take place on Friday, April 20. Truman arrived on that makeup date and promptly performed his duty of throwing out the first ball, which he did left handed while wearing a baseball glove on his right hand. Truman was known to throw right handed on these occasions as well.

The toss was caught by visiting Yankee Allie Reynolds, who then took it over to Truman to sign. The president, who had just ousted General MacArthur the week before was booed by the crowd. He was unfazed, however, as he and Mrs. Truman ate hot dogs and drank hot chocolate during the game, which was won by the home-town Senators 5-3.

Team patriarch Griffith recalled for reporters his first A.L. opener back in 1901 when he managed the Chicago White Sox. It was tradition back then for the manager and his team to walk out to the flagpole in pre-game ceremonies to raise the flag as the band struck up tunes such as "There'll be a hot time in the old town tonight."

Griffith's long-ago team the Chicago White Sox kicked off their home season also on April 20. American League president Will Harridge was the honored guest, and in recognition of the league's 50th anniversary, threw out a special gold commemorative ball in the pre-game activities. This was also the day on which the White Sox formally unveiled their new pin-striped home uniforms, which appeared to be an attempt to capture some of the success that the Yankees had attained while so attired. The Phillies had adopted the pinstriped look in 1950 and promptly went to the World Series.

As the 1951 season began to unfold, there were many developing stories and turns of events. The Giants' 2-13 start had many wondering if they had been drastically overrated in the spring and that they may have been playing over their heads during their surge at the end of the 1950 season. After winning two of their first three games of '51, everyone connected with the organization, as well as writers and fans were shocked when they lost eleven straight, including five to rival Brooklyn. Nothing seemed to be working properly, as the Giants were slumping at bat, on the mound, and defensively. Durocher insisted the problems were of a psychological nature. Usually sure-handed catcher Wes Westrum, who had made only one error in 139 games in 1950, made three in the first week of the season. He then broke a finger on May 1 and was replaced by backup Ray Noble.

After a few defensive lapses in the outfield in late April, there was even talk that the team was considering rushing 19-year-old center fielder Willie Mays up from Minneapolis of the American Association. Mays had just made his debut with the Millers on April 18. His future counterpart, Mickey Mantle, had already opened the season with the Yankees and was serving daily as the starting right fielder. Mantle's Yankees were given a boost a week after the season began when Bobby Brown was able to leave his internship to join the team. Also, Billy Martin was granted a hardship discharge at the same time from Fort Ord, California, due to the fact that he supported his mother, stepfather, and three siblings.

Just a week-and-a-half after the season began, a big three-way trade was pulled off in the A.L. between Chicago, Cleveland, and Philadelphia. The Athletics received outfielders Gus Zernial and Dave Philley, backup catcher Ray Murray, and pitcher Sam Zoldak. The White Sox got Orestes "Minnie" Minoso and Paul Lehner. Cleveland landed big left-handed pitcher Lou Brissie, who had revealed in Spring Training that his training regimen included drinking a quart of buttermilk a day. Cleveland writer Art Morrow had written of the trade: "The Athletics, Indians, and White Sox spun 'A tale of Three Cities' last week, and baseball fans everywhere found it as intriguing as anything Charles Dickens ever wrote."

Minoso paid immediate dividends for the White Sox and gave an indication of the marvelously exciting player he would be for years to come. On the first day he reported to the team, May 1, he slugged a 425-foot home run off the Yankees Vic Raschi in his first at-bat, which was the first homer of his distinguished major league career. Late in Spring Training, Cleveland writer Hal Lebovitz wrote, "On the bases, Minoso demonstrates lightning speed. His throws appear to be jet-propelled."

Oscar Ruhl added at the time of the trade, "Minoso leads the league in gold teeth with three." Just days after Minnie arrived, Chicago embarked on a span in which they won 25 of 29 games. They went on to spend a considerable portion of the season at or near the top of the American League. The race was so tight by mid-summer that on July 20, only five percentage points separated the top four teams. It would be no match however for the excitement and drama provided by the National League at the very conclusion of its race.

3

FROM COMMERCE TO THE BRONX

IN MID-APRIL OF 1951, a 19-year-old young man was poised to accomplish what was almost unheard of in the annals of the great New York Yankee dynasty.

Mickey Charles Mantle had so impressed team management with his raw skill and speed that he was set to make the jump from lowly Class C baseball to a starting berth in the Yankee Stadium outfield. Young Mantle had hailed from Commerce, Oklahoma, a zinc and lead mining town located in the northwest corner of the state, less than ten miles from both the Missouri and Kansas borders. He had spent the 1950 season playing shortstop for the Joplin, Missouri team of the Western Association, earning the modest sum of $225 per month. Mickey's abilities at shortstop were highly questionable, and he himself admitted later that he was shaky—his 55 errors in '50 seemingly supporting this assessment. His ability to run and hit were not, however, as he captured the league batting title with a .383 average and also led the league in hits, runs, and total bases.

MICKEY MANTLE. *A 19-year-old Mantle is set to begin his storybook career with the mighty New York Yankees.*

Mantle was thought by some to be the number-one minor league prospect in the country. His manager at Joplin, Harry Craft, an outfielder for the Reds in the 1930s and 40s suggested to the Yankees that he be switched to the outfield. At the conclusion of Joplin's minor league season, Yankee management allowed Mantle to travel with the major league squad for the final two weeks of the season, taking batting and fielding practice before games.

After the season, Mickey was promoted to the winter roster of Binghamton of the Class C Eastern League, where it was thought he would open the 1951 season. In mid-January, Mantle was playing guard on an independent basketball team in the Joplin Open League to keep in shape, but was ordered to stop by Yankee management to prevent the risk of injury. At the same time, Mantle was working in the zinc mines with his father several hundred feet below ground earning $33.50 per week. On February 17, he was honored as Oklahoma's # 1 rookie at the fifth annual banquet of the Old-Timers Baseball Association of Oklahoma at the Mayo Hotel in Tulsa. At the same banquet, future teammate Allie Reynolds received an award for being the state's outstanding major leaguer of 1950.

The Yankees requested that Mantle attend a preliminary camp in mid-February in Phoenix before Spring Training officially opened along with several other hopefuls.

When Mantle failed to arrive for the beginning of the early session, Yanks executive Johnny Nuen sent a telegram on February 17 asking of his whereabouts. Mantle replied that it takes money to travel, and no plane ticket was ever sent to him. The oversight was immediately rectified, and Mantle arrived in Phoenix on February 19, checking into the Continental Hotel. Joining Mickey at the preliminary camp to be looked at by Casey Stengel were second baseman Gil McDougald, MVP of the Texas League in 1950; future drinking buddy Billy Martin; college football star Jackie Jensen; and Bill "Moose" Skowron, to name a few.

For the first few days, Mantle was placed under the tutelage of longtime Yankee shortstop Frank Crosetti, who would be working with him on the finer points of defensive play in the infield. It wasn't long, however, before Stengel had Mantle taking instruction in the outfield from coach Tommy Henrich. Henrich was also acting as a batting instructor in camp, along with veteran Johnny Mize, who would still be active as a player for two more seasons. Mize was only ten months younger than Mantle's father.

By early March it had officially been decided to switch Mantle from shortstop to the outfield. Stengel said at this time that Mickey was big-league at bat and speed-wise, and he put Henrich in charge of him to help turn him into a big-league outfielder. When Joe DiMaggio indicated during his first week at Spring Training that '51 might be his last season, Stengel asked Henrich to step up the transition. Dan Daniel wrote that week: "There are scouts who say he is the next DiMaggio of the Bombers." In another article published in the March 21 issue of *The Sporting News* entitled "Mantle, 19, Tutored for DiMag Role", Stengel was quoted as saying, "To make a first-class shortstop out of Mantle would require a couple of years anyway, but to convert the young man into an outfielder— well, that should not take too long." Said Mantle of the move: "I like the idea of shifting to the outfield. It is not as tough as the infield, and out there I get a chance to use my legs."

Mickey also got what was likely his first national exposure as a Yankee when the March 7 issue of *The Sporting News* published a photo of him on page two sliding into a base at training camp.

The Yankee exhibition schedule began on March 10 versus the Cleveland Indians at Tucson. The nineteen-year-old former zinc miner from a small town in Oklahoma found himself in the Yankees starting lineup, playing center field and batting fourth. It was a reasonably successful debut as he had three hits in five trips to the plate, including a double, two runs scored, and a stolen base. Mantle was allowed to play center field in the first several Spring games as DiMaggio was breaking in slowly by only pinch hitting.

In the second game of the Spring on March 11, Mantle found that one of the finer points of outfield play was not quite as easy as DiMaggio made it appear. A high fly ball hit by Ray Boone early in the game went out to center field and hung up in the bright Phoenix sky, and as Mantle flipped his sunglasses down a bit late, the ball hit him in the forehead.

Shaken up with a bump over his left eye, he was removed from the game but returned to the lineup the next day. Mickey showed no ill effects as he went three for five against Cleveland with two runs scored and an RBI. Eventually DiMaggio took his spot in center field and Mantle moved over to right.

Mickey got his first look at the West Coast as the Yankees embarked in mid-March on an 11-day tour of California to play several exhibition games. He made quite an impression with his bat, and was the most talked-about young player with sports writers in Los Angeles and San Francisco wanting to know all about him. On March 17 at L.A.'s Wrigley Field against the local Pacific Coast League team, he hit his first home run of the spring. It was a 430-foot three-run shot that bounced off the center field wall that went farther than anyone could remember seeing a hit to that part of the park. Nine years later, he would be slugging home runs out of this same park in several episodes of the television show "Home Run Derby".

Mantle also created excitement on March 26 when the Yankees beat the University of Southern California team in Los Angeles 15-1. He contributed by hitting two home runs, a triple, and driving in seven runs. One of the homers was believed to have traveled over five hundred feet.

While on the West Coast, Mickey had the chance to enjoy himself a bit off the field as well. When the team was in Hollywood for a game against the Pacific Coast League's stars, they got to tour the Twentieth Century Fox movie studios as guests of George Jessel. On March 24, the day after the Yankees beat the San Francisco Seals 18-5, Joe D. and his brother Tom held a dinner for the team at DiMaggio's Restaurant on Fisherman's Wharf. Dan Daniel had written an article on Mantle around this time entitled "Two-Way Slugger Fitted for Clipper's Shoes."

The Yankee Clipper himself said this of his young teammate seventeen years his junior: "Mickey Mantle is the greatest prospect I can remember. Maybe he has to learn something about catching a fly ball, but that's all. He can do everything else. If he's good enough to take my job, I can always move over to left or right." Stengel added "The kid is the kind of player a manager runs into about once in his career if he's lucky." General Manager George Weiss still preferred that Mantle learn to play center field with a bit more time in the minors, perhaps under Harry Craft, now managing Beaumont, or Kansas City with George Selkirk. He was having a bit of trouble with balls hit over his head, but was learning quickly. After making such a good showing thus far, the Binghamton idea was scrapped, and Mickey signed a Kansas City contract on March 28. He was even getting the attention of Madison Avenue, as a large advertising firm offered him $1,500 to endorse products.

The Yankees were back in Phoenix on March 27 to begin a span of two games against the White Sox and two against the Cubs. Mantle continued to hit and score runs, but was forced to sit out a few games in early April due to a sprained wrist, a strained right forearm, and a bruised left hand. On April 4, the Yankees had traveled to El Paso, Texas and beat that city's local Southwest International League team 16-10 in a game that saw both DiMaggio and Mantle hit home runs, Mantle's being his sixth of the spring.

When Mickey phoned home that day, his father informed him that he had received word that the draft-eligible 19-year-old was to report to his draft board in Miami, Oklahoma on April 11. He had already been declared 4-F by this same board in December due to a condition known as osteomyelitis—an inflammation in a bone in his left ankle caused originally by a football injury in high school. Mickey had been hospitalized four times during his teens with the condition, with each stay lasting about two weeks. It was even feared at one time that he might lose a portion of his leg. Nevertheless, his local draft board felt the need to examine him further to reconsider his status.

At this time, a couple of baseball writers made glittering projections regarding Mantle. Chicago writer Ed Burns, who had observed him during the White Sox and Cubs exhibitions wrote that the Yankees would retain their World Championship in '51, in part due to the addition of Mantle. Jimmy Powers, sports editor of the *New York Daily News* predicted that he would be the Rookie of the Year for 1951.

The Yankees played exhibition games against the Boston Braves on April 10 in Dallas and April 11 in Kansas City. Mantle's family drove to Kansas City to see the game, and Mickey returned with them in order to attend his appointment with the draft board. His 4-F status was subsequently reaffirmed. It had actually been observed by many in camp that Mantle walked with a slight limp, even though it was undetectable when he ran.

When Mantle returned to the team after his appointment with the draft board, they were set to travel home to New York to take on the Brooklyn Dodgers in one final three-game exhibition series. When Stengel was asked about Mickey's status, he snapped "Don't question me about Mantle. It is too early to discuss him as a fixture."

Of all the rookies in Spring Training with the Yankees, only Mantle, Gil McDougald, and pitcher Tom Morgan remained with the team when camp broke. As it became evident that Mantle would be opening the season on the Yankees' major league roster, Stengel made the following statement:

"Promoting a 19-year-old boy from Class C to the Yankees is something of a historic occasion. We would not have done it if we were not convinced that Mickey could make it. He is amazingly fast. He can hit for extra bases from either side of the plate; is improving vastly as an outfielder, whereas at the outset of the training season he was a shortstop, and is the type of ballplayer you may run into perhaps once in a generation."

Regarding Mantle's speed, Yankee scout Tom Greenwade had put the stopwatch on him during a game in Joplin when he had hit a triple. From the time he touched first base until he hit third came in at just under six seconds.

The Yankees-Dodgers exhibition series was set to begin at Yankee Stadium on Friday, April 13. It was the following day at Ebbets Field that Mantle appeared in a game for the first time within the New York City limits, managing just one hit on the afternoon. That evening, he and his teammates attended the wedding reception of Whitey Ford in Long Island City.

In the final exhibition on Sunday, Mantle put on a show for the Ebbets Field crowd with a home run and three singles. That Sunday evening after the final Dodger game, he got a bit of exposure off the field as he and his mentor, coach Henrich, appeared on "The Big Show" starring Tallulah Bankhead. Afterward, the team boarded the New York-Washington Express train to D.C. for the season opener versus the Senators the following afternoon, April 16. Yankee owners Del Webb and Dan Topping were making the trip, and a conversation was held in the train's smoking lounge in which Stengel convinced them to sign Mantle to a $7,500 contract for '51.

Mickey and his mates spent that night and most of the next day at Washington's Shoreham Hotel, as the opener on Monday was postponed due to rain. That evening they trekked back to New York City to prepare for their home opener against the Red Sox on Tuesday. In his first few days in the city, Mantle was rooming by himself at the Concourse Plaza Hotel—a long way from Commerce, Oklahoma indeed.

Mantle was about to officially begin his major league career with a starting assignment in right field of Yankee Stadium versus Ted Williams and the Boston Red Sox. Before the game, he sat on a stool in front of his locker and looked somewhat bewildered. For much of his youth, he had read stories of the DiMaggio brothers, Williams, Bob Feller, and all the rest, but it was he who would be playing alongside the great Joltin' Joe himself.

Sporting News Editor J.G. Taylor Spink published a few of Mantle's thoughtful comments from those moments a short time before the opening game in his publication's April 25th issue:

> "I somehow get the feeling that I hadn't ought to be here, that maybe it's a mistake, after all, I am supposed to be in Kansas City. Now Mr. Spink, please do not misunderstand this statement. I do not lack confidence. If I did, I would not be sitting here with you, a Yankee. It's just that I am awed by the history of the New York club and by my company."

With that, young Mantle took his place in the Stadium's right field, wearing the number six on his pinstriped Yankee uniform. Prominently placed in the third spot in the batting order in front of DiMaggio, Mickey came away with his first official hit, RBI, and run scored in the 5-0 shutout over the rival Red Sox. That milestone first hit was a single between shortstop and third base off lefty Bill Wight which scored Jackie Jensen. While playing defense in right field, Mickey looked to DiMaggio for help. He admitted after that, "Joe tells me where to play the batters. I study Joe all the while. I marvel at his speed at 36. I marvel at his grace and nonchalance." Mantle asked a reporter regarding Joe D., "Have you ever seen anybody better?" When Mantle himself was told that he appeared to be taking everything in stride, he replied, "I cannot afford to get a swelled head. I would not be able to go back home. They don't like swelled heads in my section of Oklahoma. I couldn't face my pals."

Mantle capped off the evening of his debut by attending a Welcome Home dinner for the Yankees in the Grand Ballroom of the Hotel Concourse. The affair was thrown by a local civic organization known as the People of the Bronx, with 500 guests on hand.

Back to work in right field the next afternoon, Mantle watched pitcher Eddie Lopat take a no-hitter into the seventh inning. With one out, Ted Williams broke it up with a single, but the Yanks still prevailed 6-1. Mickey chipped in with a two-run single off Ellis Kinder in the eighth inning.

The Yankees traveled back down to Washington on April 19 to make up the postponed opener as part of a doubleheader the next day. It was that day that Mickey was able to witness President Truman performing his duty of throwing out the first ball at Griffith Stadium. New York dropped both games, and Mantle, who batted in the cleanup spot only went one for ten on the day. The one hit he did manage was his first major league triple, driving in a run.

The next few games, Stengel inserted Mantle into the leadoff spot, and he was a factor in two games the Yankees won by one run. On April 21, one of his two hits was an eighth-inning double that drove in Rizzuto with the winning run. Two days later, he had three singles against the Athletics in New York, one which drove in the tying run just before he scored the winning run.

When the Yankees got to Boston to begin a series on April 26, Stengel decided to sit Mantle, having gone zero for eight in his last few games. The manager said of Fenway Park, "Right field here is too big and too sunny." Mantle was utilized as a pinch hitter in the ninth inning but struck out. The next day he was given the starting assignment in left field, one of the few times in his career he would man the position.

When the Yankees set out for a western road trip on April 30, Stengel informed Mickey that he was, in a manner of speaking, putting him on probation for the next couple of weeks. He had only hit .222 thus far at home, and had only two hits in his last 20 at-bats overall. Stengel lectured Mantle on failing to take full advantage of his remarkable speed—especially in the field—telling the youngster, "You can outrun any player in the majors, but one would not get that impression watching you in the field. Put on a show. Be more dramatic." It was believed that if Mantle failed to begin making a better impression, he would be sent down to Kansas City.

In the first game of the road trip, May 1 in Chicago, Mantle got his first look at Comiskey Park and posted a very important career milestone that day. In the Yankees' 8-3 win, Mickey connected in the sixth inning for home run number one of 536 off White Sox pitcher Randy Gumpert. Another noteworthy rookie and future star, Minnie Minoso, recently acquired by the White Sox, also slugged his first career home run in this game. The 425-foot blow came in his first at-bat with Chicago in the first inning off Vic Raschi.

Three days later at Sportsman's Park in St. Louis, Mantle tagged his second homer, a mammoth 450-foot blast off Duane Pillette that carried over the right-field roof and across Grand Ave. Batting now in the leadoff spot temporarily, Mantle really caught fire in the first week of May despite a strained right hand. In the five games from May 3 through May 7, he had at least two hits each game, going 12 for 25 with nine runs scored and seven RBI.

Around this time, Yankee management made a couple of decisions regarding Mantle. They requested that he refrain from making television and radio appearances so that he could concentrate strictly on baseball; and when rosters were to be cut down from 28 to 25 on May 17, Mantle would be staying with the major league squad. Dan Daniel wrote in his column in late May that Mantle still tries to belt the ball out of the park every time he's not bunting. Stengel had ordered him to be on the field every morning at 11 A.M., ready for instruction when the team was at home. He would be getting an hour-and-a-half of special tutoring from Stengel, Henrich, and Bill Dickey, and even bunting tips from Phil Rizzuto.

In late May and early June, Mantle had slumped badly, and Stengel was starting to get concerned. In addition, he had a sprained left hand that prevented him from swinging properly. Pitchers were also discovering that he could be pitched on the inside part of the plate. In a series against the Red Sox in Boston at the end of May, he had gone zero for nine, which included five strikeouts in a Memorial Day doubleheader. His father, Elvin, even came to Detroit in early June to see him play and to give him a pep talk.

The Tigers fans were unmerciful to Mick during the series, hurling insults and even whiskey bottles at one point. One Yankee beat writer who traveled with the team suggested that they give Mickey a week off so that he could go back to Oklahoma to marry his fiance Merlyn Johnson, figuring that might be a calming influence. Mickey actually had planned to do so early in the season, but was convinced by management that at 19 he shouldn't rush into it.

Several games later, on June 6 in St. Louis, when Mantle tripled after striking out his first two times up, he had broken a 0 for 23 streak. The only day in the entire month of June on which he truly stood out came during a doubleheader on the 19th against the White Sox at the Stadium. In the opener Mantle went three for four with a home run, four RBI, two runs scored, and a stolen base. In Game Two he added another home run. Removing that one day from the equation, Mickey's month of June included no home runs and a .200 batting average in 70 at-bats.

The small-town boy was becoming a bit disillusioned with big-league life in the big city. Oscar Ruhl wrote in his *Sporting News* column in the July 4 issue that Mantle didn't trust people as much as he used to, and added:

"Five months ago he was making $33.90 a week in the mine. Once, he was eager to answer questions. Now he avoids them. He is disturbed by fan mail, and the girls, and the subway rides. He feels as though he is being pushed around."

Things were simply not going well for Mickey on or off the field. Beginning with a June 27 game in Washington in which he was benched in favor of Hank Bauer, Mantle began a stretch of two-and-a-half weeks in which he saw precious little playing time. In the 15 games New York played in that span, he saw no action in seven, and had one pinch-hitting appearance each in four others. The 15 official at-bats he totaled yielded only three hits. Probably the highlight for him during this period didn't involve him directly, but came when he played in Allie Reynolds' no-hitter against the Indians on July 12. Oscar Ruhl wrote that Stengel has changed his tune on Mantle. "He used to say, 'He's a good ball player', but now he says, 'He's GOING to be a good ball player.' "

The decision to give Mantle more seasoning at the minor league level came on Sunday, July 15, while the team was in Detroit. A roster move was made necessary when the team had purchased left-handed pitcher Art Shallock from the Hollywood Stars of the Pacific Coast League. Some saw the move as an indication that the Yankees knew DiMaggio would not be an everyday player in 1952, and that Mantle needed work in center field in order to be his replacement.

As Stengel informed him of the decision at Briggs Stadium before a doubleheader with the Tigers, Mickey became teary-eyed and left the park immediately. He then joined the Kansas City Blues of the American Association. At the time of his demotion. Mickey was batting .260 with seven homers and 45 RBI. Management felt that with his speed he should always be able to get on base at least once per game by bunting, but despite much instruction in the art, he still didn't seem to pick it up. He had continued to swing too hard, trying to murder the ball, which led to too many strikeouts. Said Stengel of the demotion, which was believed to be for the duration of the season:

"Shipping Mantle to Kansas City involved a very tough decision. Mantle is a remarkable player in the making. I don't believe that anybody doubts this . . . . He will be a regular on the New York club to stay, in time."

Mantle joined Kansas City in Milwaukee for his first game on July 16. The Blues were managed by longtime Yankee outfielder George Selkirk, who followed Stengel's wishes and inserted Mantle in center field. Kansas City fans hoped that the arrival of Mantle would not mean the promotion of center fielder Bob Cerv, who was having an outstanding offensive season. Cerv would remain for the time being, and was merely shifted to right field.

Mantle did little in his first few games in a Kansas City uniform to distinguish himself, and some fans were abusive toward him, even calling him a "draft dodger." He got very down on himself, and when the team arrived back in Kansas City, his first game at Blues Stadium did not help improve the situation. Facing Minneapolis starter Hoyt Wilhelm, himself a season away from his debut with the New York Giants, Mickey was hitless in three at-bats.

It was at this time that his father came to visit him at the Aladdin Hotel in Kansas City, and Mantle often later told of him angrily packing Mick's suitcase saying, "I thought I raised a man, not a coward!" Mickey convinced his father that things would get better, and very soon, they did. On July 21 he went four for six with a triple and two runs scored. The last five days of the month he began to rediscover his power, with six home runs in cities such as Louisville, Indianapolis, and Toledo. July 31 in particular was a highlight, going five for five with two homers, a single, double, and a triple, with three RBI and three runs scored. That day, the Yankees did promote Cerv up to the big-league roster, while Jackie Jensen would be joining Mickey in the Kansas City outfield. Jensen played right field and batted cleanup behind Mantle, who almost always hit third during his time with K.C.

The team was faced with the oddity of playing three straight doubleheaders on August 3, 4, and 5. Mantle tested the patience of Selkirk in the August 4 twin-bill as he dropped a ball in center that allowed three runs to score, as well as misplaying a few others.

He redeemed himself in the eighth inning by driving in two runs for a 7-5 win. The following night, in what may have been a punishment, he found himself playing left field.

Mantle's military eligibility became an issue yet again, as the White House revealed on August 3 that it had received three letters protesting his 4-F status. For the third time in nine months he was notified to report for a physical, specifically to have Army doctors re-examine his left leg. Mantle said of the notice, "If I have to take another physical, it's okay, and if I have to go into the service, I'll just have to go." The examination was scheduled for August 20.

In the second and third weeks of August, he had several productive games; two hits and three RBI on the 7th versus Indianapolis; four hits, three RBIs, and two stolen bases against Louisville. In a four-game span from August 13 through August 15, which included one doubleheader, Mickey was 10 for 18 with four homers, 11 RBIs, and five runs scored. He was clearly demonstrating to Yankee management that he was worth another look, and his dues-paying days in the minor leagues were about to come to a close.

On Friday, August 17, before a game in which the Blues were hosting Toledo, many player participation events were held, including an egg-catching contest, fungo hitting, outfield relay throwing, a blindfolded wheelbarrow race, etc. It came as no surprise that Mantle won the home run derby.

Two days later, the Kansas City fans got their last look at Mickey in Blues jersey No. 12 during a Sunday doubleheader against Toledo. That afternoon he had two hits, including a double in the opener, and closed out his minor league career with a home run in Game Two. Mantle was officially recalled by the Yankees the next day, August 20, and his final statistics with K.C. showed that in 40 games, he had 11 home runs, 45 RBIs, and an impressive .364 batting average. He left Kansas City and reported to the draft board at Fort Sill, Oklahoma, with yet again the same rejection results.

Mantle rejoined the Yankees on August 24 and appeared in the starting lineup batting second. His promotion meant the demotion of Cerv, who was sent back to Kansas City after a relatively unsuccessful three-week stint with New York.

In Mantle's four at-bats that Friday in Cleveland, he managed one single in the Yanks' 2-0 win and was replaced by Hank Bauer late in the game. More importantly, he was back in the big leagues to stay. Settling back into New York City, Mantle moved into an apartment with Bauer and Johnny Hopp on 7th Ave. over the Stage Delicatessen in midtown Manhattan. Mickey looked up to Bauer, who was nearly ten years his senior and tough as nails. Hank had spent nearly three years in the Pacific during World War II, and earned two Purple Hearts and two Bronze Stars.

The day after his return Mickey helped to justify his promotion with a home run, a double, two RBIs, and two runs scored in New York's 7-3 win over the Indians. Four days later in St. Louis, now batting in the leadoff spot, his four RBIs included a three-run home run off Satchel Paige in the ninth inning.

Mantle would spend the majority of September as the team's leadoff hitter. His first big highlight of the month came on the 8th in Eddie Lopat's 4-0 shutout over Washington. The game was scoreless until the seventh inning when Mick hit a prodigious 450-foot three-run homer to contribute greatly to the win. He followed up the next day with a solo shot in a 7-5 win over the Senators in Game One of a twin bill. Ten days later his final home run of the season was the difference in the Yanks' 5-3 win over Chicago.

Mantle was on the bench on September 28, the day New York clinched its third straight A.L. pennant by beating the Red Sox. He would now cap off his roller coaster ride of a rookie season with the opportunity to appear in the spotlight of the World Series. In the 96 games he had appeared in for the Yankees in his debut season, Mantle recorded a .267 batting average in 341 official at-bats. He connected for 13 home runs and drove in 65 runs. On the eve of the beginning of the World Series, Stengel showed some regret for not allowing Mantle the chance to further add to those figures. He stated "One of my biggest mistakes was shipping (him) to Kansas City for the middle third of the season. He should have been with us all through the campaign. He would have made things a bit easier for me."

Mantle would play his first of what would turn out to be 65 career World Series games on October 4, very fittingly at home at Yankee Stadium. He led off for the Yanks in the bottom of the first against lefty Dave Koslo and flied out to right field. In his five plate appearances he reached base twice via walks and had the misfortune of flying out to another youngster making his World Series debut, Willie Mays, to end the game.

The next afternoon as the Yankees attempted to even up the Series, an incident occurred that was very noteworthy in the career of Mickey Mantle. The game started on a positive enough note as he led off the Yankee first inning by laying down an excellent bunt that allowed him to reach first base safely. A couple batters later he scored on a single to give the Yanks a 1-0 lead. They added a run in the second inning and took a 2-0 lead into the bottom of the third, as Mantle was struck out by Larry Jansen to lead off that frame.

Moving ahead to the top of the fifth inning, Mays led off and lofted a fly ball to right center field. Stengel had told Mantle before the game to take every ball that came that way as DiMaggio's heel was bothering him. As Mantle pursued the fly, he realized that DiMaggio was nearby, and as he gave way to the legend, he twisted his right knee severely when he caught it on a drain cover. DiMaggio made the catch and immediately rushed over to Mickey, who was writhing in pain on the ground. Joe told him not to move, and that a stretcher would be coming out to get him.

This would turn out to be the first in a series of injuries that would plague him throughout his career. When he got to the clubhouse, the knee was packed in ice and team doctor Sidney Gaynor had him sent to Lenox Hill Hospital. Mantle's father, who was in the crowd, accompanied him to the hospital. As his father was attempting to assist him in from the sidewalk into the building, the elder Mantle collapsed himself. Father and son ended up sharing the same hospital room, and though the press initially reported that the Elvin Mantle had suffered a back injury, he was subsequently diagnosed with Hodgkin's Disease.

After surgery to repair damaged ligaments, Mickey watched the rest of the Series on television as his teammates clinched the

World Championship on October 10. He then went home to Oklahoma for the winter to recuperate. With his share of World Series money—over $6,000—he bought a more spacious house in Commerce for his family around this time.

On Halloween night, 11 days after he celebrated his 20th birthday, Mantle made news when he was involved in an auto mishap. He was driving about a mile south of Baxter Springs, Kansas and was forced to drive into a ditch to avoid a collision with an oncoming car. He managed to escape uninjured, and there was only slight damage to his car, which had to be towed out. Around the same time, Mantle joined Mays in being named to *The Sporting News* Major League All-Rookie Team.

In mid-November, Mantle was still having difficulty walking without a brace on his right leg. On November 13 he visited Dr. Phog Allen, an osteopath who was also the basketball coach at the University of Kansas. Mickey reported that he wasn't doing anything other than a little duck hunting, and said "....the knee feels real weak." In early December, the Yankees brought Mantle to New York to be examined. He was given a smaller brace to wear for the next few weeks, and was also fitted with a weighted boot to exercise with once the smaller brace was discarded. Both Dr. Gaynor as well as Dr. George Bennett of Johns Hopkins assured Yankee management that Mickey would be fit to resume playing come Spring Training. Mantle left New York to return home on December 4.

On December 17, Mickey and his fiance Merlyn were issued a marriage license in Miami, Oklahoma, and married six days later at her parents' home in nearby Picher.

More had occurred to the young country boy in the previous ten months than he could have ever possibly imagined. And yet the coming years would make his 1951 season seem almost modest by comparison, as he was destined to fulfill virtually every positive expectation that was held.

4

STARS COME OUT IN MOTOR CITY

THE EIGHTEENTH ANNUAL MID-SUMMER CLASSIC OF 1951 had originally been scheduled to take place at Shibe Park in Philadelphia, with the Phillies acting as the host team. In light of the city of Detroit celebrating the 250th anniversary of its founding, Tigers owner Walter O. Briggs had requested of Phillies owner Robert Carpenter that it be switched to the Michigan city to be included as part of the celebration, to which Carpenter graciously agreed. Briggs subsequently showed his gratitude by taking out a full page ad in *The Sporting News* to thank him.

It had been ten years since Detroit had hosted the 1941 game—one in which the lasting highlight was a game-winning three-run home run by Ted Williams in the bottom of the ninth inning for an American League victory. Ted was now still troubled by the elbow he had broken in the 1950 All-Star Game making a great catch off Ralph Kiner and banging hard into the outfield wall of Comiskey Park. Despite the still-ailing elbow, which caused him to miss the rest of the '50 campaign, Ted had drawn the starting assignment this year in left field.

It was the fans who had the responsibility of selecting the starting team in '51, through a vote conducted by newspapers, magazines, and radio stations. Stan Musial had the distinction of garnering more votes than any other player that summer with 1,428,283. It was written after the votes were tallied that even if the players had done the voting, Stan would have been "the man" amongst them as well.

Under the A.L.'s revised rules in '51 for the selection of the All-Star teams, the manager was obligated to pick one pitcher from each team in the league. As a result, A.L. manager Casey Stengel had to pass up deserving pitchers such as Bob Feller and his own hurlers Vic Raschi and Allie Reynolds, in favor of Bob Lemon and Eddie Lopat.

The Eighteenth Classic on July 10 was to be broadcast over 545 radio stations coast to coast, as well as by shortwave radio to occupation troops overseas and Naval ships at sea. Mel Allen of the Yankees and Art Helfer of the Dodgers would be calling the action. Tiger great Ty Cobb, returning to the scene of so much of his former glory, performed the duty of tossing out the first ball, which was received by Browns pitcher Ned Garver. Sitting in the box with Cobb was outgoing commissioner "Happy" Chandler, as well as his former teammate and future Hall of Famer Sam Crawford.

A capacity crowd of 52,075 had turned out, and Tigers general manager Billy Evans said the game could have drawn 120,000 if the stadium could have accommodated them.

"We turned back applications for at least 70,000 seats we do not possess." As it was, the attendance generated $124,294 for the Players Pension Fund.

Right hander Garver started the game for the A.L., opposed by fellow righty Robin Roberts of the Phillies. On Garver's first delivery of the game, the Phils' Richie Ashburn doubled to left field. Later in the inning with two outs and Ashburn on third base, Musial attempted to steal second. Yogi Berra's throw was on time, but Nellie Fox dropped the ball as Ashburn scampered home with the first run. The A.L. got the run back in the second inning when Berra singled and scored on Ferris Fain's triple.

Going into the top of the third, the game was still tied at one, and Garver was relieved by lefty Lopat. The Yanks hurler immediately ran into trouble when Musial led off with a homer into the upper deck in right field. Two batters later, Gil Hodges singled, and the Braves' Bob Elliot drove him in with a home run to left for a 4-1 N.L. lead. Lopat finished the inning, and Berra admitted later that his teammate had pitched terribly. "It's a good thing he wasn't pitching in a game," said professor Yogi.

It was then the A.L.'s turn for the long ball, as hometown Tiger Vic Wertz thrilled the fans with a solo shot in the bottom of the fourth. Fellow Tiger George Kell did the same off Maglie in the fifth to cut the margin to 4-3. Detroit pitcher Fred Hutchinson wasn't so lucky, as he allowed a two-run blast to Gil Hodges in the sixth, and a run-scoring squeeze bunt to Jackie Robinson in the seventh. In the eighth inning, Ralph Kiner closed out the scoring with a solo home run off Boston lefty Mel Parnell. It was the third consecutive year that slugger Kiner had homered in the All-Star Game. The contest ended 8-3 in favor of the N.L., with Maglie credited with the win; Lopat was charged with the loss.

After watching the N.L.'s power display, Eddie Sawyer of the Phillies who managed the team said, "I'd like to fool around with this squad all summer." Ted Williams, who injured himself in the game for the second year in a row, this time while sliding, voiced his dissatisfaction later to Shirley Povich of the *Washington Post* regarding the makeup of the A.L. squad:

> "I didn't like our lineup in the All-Star Game. All of 'em are nice fellows, but we were trying to beat the National with too many leadoff and second-place hitters in our batting order. In the All-Star Game you got to load up with the big guys. The fans who vote pay too much attention to averages and not enough to the long ball."

The N.L.'s win—its second in a row, marked the first time in the history of the exhibition that the circuit had won back-to-back games. Ford Frick, who had served as N.L. president since the second year of the inter-league contest was jubilant, saying, "I hate to recall how long I've waited for these two straight victories."

For the next 14 years, Frick would have to maintain neutrality, at least publicly.

5

A GREAT DAY
FOR SLUGGERS

ON A SUNNY SUMMER DAY, JULY 23, 1951, the
National Baseball Hall of Fame would be welcoming two new members into its ranks—two men who had combined for a total of 1,045
home runs throughout their lengthy, distinguished major league
careers. Perennial home run leaders Jimmie Foxx and Mel Ott officially became the 59th and 60th members of baseball's hallowed
shrine that day.

The results of the 1951 election conducted by the Baseball
Writers Association of America were made public on January 26,
and revealed that with 170 votes required for induction, Ott garnered 197, while Foxx received 179. Respected sportswriter Arthur
Daley had made an impassioned plea for the election of Ott in his
New York Times column of January 14, which may have helped put
him over the top. Ott, who led the N.L. in homers four times on
the way to a total of 511, was notified of his election that day while
visiting an institution called the Marine Leprosarium. He responded,
"I'm tickled to death."

Foxx, whose 534 home runs placed him second behind only
Babe Ruth, was a salesman for a trucking firm in Doylestown, Penn-

sylvania. When contacted, he said he was "delighted by such an honor." Living in a new home in the Maplewood section of Doylestown, about 30 miles from Philadelphia, Foxx reflected at this time on a few prominent events of his career. He said that until he received the news of his election, the one moment that stood out in his mind was hitting a home run off Burleigh Grimes of the Cardinals to win Game Five of the 1930 World Series for the Athletics.

One disappointment he experienced was not breaking Babe Ruth's single-season home run record in 1932, finishing two shy with 58. "Had the right-field fence in Shibe Park been the same for me as it was for Babe, I would have had the new record." In '32, there was barbed wire on top of the right-field fence, which Foxx hit three times for doubles.

He also compared two legendary pitchers, commenting, "I faced Walter Johnson when he was finished, and I honestly believe he was faster than Bob Feller was at his best." Foxx was able to share his views publicly that spring, starring in his own local television show called "Sports Pictorial" every Friday night at 7 P.M. on WPTZ in Philadelphia.

On Foxx's special day in Cooperstown, A.L. president Will Harridge was unable to attend due to illness, so it was Earl Hilligan, director of the American League Service Bureau who dedicated Jimmie's newly minted bronze plaque. In his introduction, Hilligan spoke of Foxx's tremendous slugging power, and recalled a home run Foxx hit at Comiskey Park on June 16, 1936 that went over a 352-foot marker in lest field, cleared the roof 90 feet above ground and landed in a playground 535 feet from home plate.

Foxx also took time at the ceremony to pose for a photograph with Connie Mack, who had been his manager for the first 11 years of his career.

Unfortunately, Mel Ott was unable to attend the proceedings due to the team he was managing, the Oakland Oaks of the Pacific Coast League being in the midst of a pennant race. National League president Ford Frick, who had delivered the principal address at the induction ceremony, also accepted Ott's plaque on his behalf, dedi-

JIMMIE FOXX AND MEL OTT. *1951 Hall of Fame inductees Jimmie Foxx and Mel Ott posed together in the late 1930s. Courtesy: Boston Public Library.*

cating it in grandiose fashion "not only to Ott, but to the players of all time, those of the past, the present and those of the future who will continue to make our game better day by day, year by year."

As part of the occasion, the tenth annual Hall of Fame Game, this year between the Dodgers and the Athletics, drew the biggest turnout to date in the history of the exhibition. Broadcast coast to coast as "Mutual's Game of the Day", the 9-4 Brooklyn win featured an exciting finish with two-run home runs each by Carl Furillo and Cal Abrams in the ninth inning.

It is worthy of mention that whereas in recent times, starting players tend to make token appearances in this annual exhibition, virtually all of the Dodgers and Athletics regulars played the entire game. Many of these same Dodger players would one day take their place in Cooperstown alongside Foxx and Ott, including Duke Snider, Roy Campanella, Pee Wee Reese, and Jackie Robinson.

One heartwarming incident occurred involving Jackie as a result of 1951's Hall of Fame game. A 14-year-old boy from Cooperstown named Johnny Nagelschmidt asked Robinson for an autograph after the game. Young Johnny handed Jackie a scorecard through the window of the team bus, and it was then passed around for others to sign. A few moments later, Johnny asked Jackie for the scorecard back, and Robinson realized that in the commotion it had been handed back to the wrong autograph seeker. Jackie then asked the lad for his name and address and assured him that he would send an autograph.

A couple of weeks later, Johnny received a baseball autographed by the entire Brooklyn team, along with a letter.

Tracked down in February 2001, John Nagelschmidt happily reflected on having acquired the prized possession 50 years before. Now 64, John is an accountant and lives in Cortland, New York. He treasures the memory of growing up in Cooperstown, attending many ceremonies, and having the opportunity to chat with the likes of Ty Cobb and Connie Mack.

Robinson became a favorite of John's, and the only thing that prevented him from attending Jackie's own induction ceremony in 1962 was not being able to get the day off from his job at Cooperstown's National Commercial Bank.

JOHN NAGLESCHMIDT. *John Nagleschmidt posed with his Brooklyn Dodgers autographed baseball he received in August of 1951. Courtesy of John Nagleschmidt.*

6

THE CIRCUS COMES TO ST. LOUIS

WHEN HE HAD PURCHASED THE CLEVE-LAND INDIANS FRANCHISE in June of 1946, Bill Veeck did so for the primary purpose of bringing a world championship to that city for the first time since 1920. Innovative and daring even then, he signed Larry Doby to break the American League color barrier in 1947, and little more than a year later brought in pitcher Satchel Paige as a 42-year-old major league rookie. When his Tribe captured the elusive World Series title against the Braves in 1948, Veeck had accomplished what he had set out to do, then lost his enthusiasm and sold the team in November of '49. "The challenge isn't there anymore," he said at the time.

The 37-year-old Veeck was a flamboyant, garrulous ex-marine who sported a pirate-like wooden leg as a result of a war injury. The handicap did not slow him down, and it also didn't prevent him from being an excellent tennis player. Bill was known for wearing fancy open-neck sport shirts and was never encumbered by a necktie.

By early 1951, it was widely known that Veeck was interested in returning to baseball. The St. Louis Browns were thought to be the kind of challenge he might take on, though in January he did deny a report that he was making an offer for the team. Struggling to make it in a city they shared with the more popular Cardinals, the Browns had drawn only 247,000 fans to Sportsman's Park during the 1950 season. Team owners, brothers Bill and Charley DeWitt, claimed they would need to draw 500,000 in '51 to meet their expenses. In the spring they borrowed $600,000 from a local bank to cover the team's debts.

There was even talk of relocating the team, and Los Angeles was thought to be an interesting site. Fred Miller, a wealthy brewer from Milwaukee was making an effort to land a major league team for his city, with a new stadium expected to be finished by the spring of '52. Miller was said to be very interested in the Browns, and when he was seen at their game on May 9 seated just a couple of boxes away from the DeWitt brothers, it fueled further speculation that a sale might be in the works.

J. Roy Stockton, sports editor of the *St. Louis Post-Dispatch* reported on May 10 that there was a plan to move the team to Milwaukee, and that Veeck was about to enter the picture and support the move. Bill DeWitt continued to deny the rumors.

Just days later on May 15, investment broker Mark Steinberg, once part-owner of the Cardinals, purchased a $700,000 note from a man named Richard Muckerman, secured by 56% of stock in the Browns. The note, due February 1, 1954 was given to Muckerman by the DeWitt brothers when they took over controlling interest in the team in 1949. Steinberg was known to be a friend of Veeck's, and it was believed that Bill had a hand in the purchase. The rumors continued that Veeck would swing a deal for control of the Browns, then either move them to Los Angeles or sell them to Miller in Milwaukee.

It became public knowledge in early June that Veeck was indeed heading a group negotiating to buy the team. It was written that if successful he would be content for the time being to give the city of St. Louis a chance to keep the Browns, though he was keeping the Los Angeles option open. He had reportedly even discussed rental terms with the L.A. Coliseum. L.A. had very nearly become the new home of the Browns ten years earlier, when then-owner Donald Barnes had made a very serious attempt to transfer the team.

Finally, after months of speculation, the word came on June 21 that Veeck and associates had tentatively agreed to buy controlling interest in the franchise, taking over as early as July 5. Veeck spoke at a press conference at the city's Hotel Jefferson that June day, and upon seeing the large crowd of newsmen, cracked, "This is a better turnout than the Browns ever had for their home games." He admitted that this was "a team that can't beat their way out of a paper bag with a crowbar." He said that he planned to revive the team "with interesting baseball and side attractions that will make the people of St. Louis want to patronize the Browns."

He also emphasized that he had no plans to move to Milwaukee, L.A., or anywhere, even in the long term, and expressed a belief that the Browns and Cardinals could coexist in St. Louis. He was asked at the press conference if it was true that he would immediately add as many as six black players to the Browns' roster. He responded that he was associated with Harlem Globetrotters owner Abe Saperstein, who also ran the Negro League's Chicago American Giants.

Veeck brought up the name of his old friend Satchel Paige, saying that he was pitching for the team that season and was having a good year. Veeck had been on hand for a doubleheader between the American Giants and the Birmingham Black Barons at Comiskey Park on May 20, with Paige the starting pitcher in the opener. Veeck received a trophy between games as an appreciation for his role in integration. Olympic gold medalist Jesse Owens had been in charge of the committee responsible for the tribute.

Veeck revealed that he had been considering making a bid for the Browns ever since he had sold the Indians. He had now acquired the 58% interest in the team that was held by the DeWitts. In order to complete the deal, Veeck would also need to acquire additional stock to give him 206,250 shares, which was 75% of the 275,000 total shares of stock. The time limit for shareholders to sell their stock at $7 per share was set at July 3.

BILL VEECK AND SATCHEL PAIGE. *Bill Veeck brought pitching great Satchel Paige back to the major leagues for the second time in July of 1951.*

Ownership groups from four other cities had entered the bidding to buy the team around this time. Veeck said that representatives from not only L.A. and Milwaukee, but also Baltimore and Queens, New York had contacted him about moving the Browns there, but he felt that making a go of it in St. Louis would be a fun challenge. An editorial on the matter in *The Sporting News* in early July quipped, "A challenge? If that's what Veeck likes, he has stepped into the ring with the champion of all challenges."

At the same time, Ed McAuley of the *Cleveland News* speculated with a fair amount of accuracy what Bill might have in store for the baseball world: "He'll trot onto the diamond the strangest collection of hired hands ever to wear big-league uniforms . . . and he'll show his audience the fresh contortions of Max Patkin . . . . " "The American League has found a financial godfather in the darkest corner of its economic tenement . . . . " On a more serious note, Veeck made it known that when he took over, the team would be completely reorganized administratively and would be operated by a newly formed corporation owned by him and his associates.

The specific requirements were ironed out, and the sale, representing an outlay of over two million dollars, was completed in early July. The first home game of the Veeck regime was Friday, July 6, with the Browns hosting the Chicago White Sox. The carnival atmosphere most had anticipated was in full force, as the fans were entertained by a clown band and a fireworks display. Veeck himself was amongst the crowd, distributing free Cokes and Falstaff beer to patrons. He had even installed chalkboards in the restrooms and invited comments and suggestions.

The following day he declared "Ladies Night" and distributed 4,290 orchids to female fans. Veeck insisted, however, that showmanship was secondary to operating a ballclub. "We're selling baseball, not side attractions," he said. His intention was to build up the farm system and add many new scouts to the payroll, and almost immediately made an unsuccessful attempt to acquire his old Indians manager, Lou Boudreau, from Boston in order to install him as his new field boss.

Veeck did comment on the growing scarcity of colorful ballplayers capable of luring big crowds at the gate. He asked, "What has become of players with crowd appeal, such as Dizzy Dean?" He said that current players like Musial, Kiner, and Hodges may rank among the game's greats, but none have tremendous crowd appeal.

Veeck then proceeded on July 14 to secure the name Satchel Paige, one of the more colorful ballplayers of the modern era, to a Browns contract. The next day, Paige made his last appearance with the American Giants against the Monarchs in Kansas City, pitching three hitless innings. He had mainly been pitching three-inning stints several times a week in the Negro Leagues, and upon his arrival said he was glad to be back in the A.L. so he could catch up on his rest. Paige revealed at this time that he was on the verge of quitting the Chicago team when Veeck's offer came. He added, "Bill Veeck promised me a long time ago that he'd send for me whenever he came back to baseball," and "I'll give it all to Bill, for he's a wonderful man to work for. I mean that— every word of it!"

Satchel made his first appearance with the Browns versus Washington at St. Louis on July 18. He started the game and lasted eight innings, giving up five runs in the 7-1 loss. Though he gave up 11 hits, many were bloopers and infield hits. When questioned after, Paige, believed to be 45 years old said, "No, I ain't afraid of a sore arm. Never had one in my life." It was, however, manager Zack Taylor's intention to primarily utilize him in a relief role.

The addition of a personality like Paige brought forth several interesting stories and incidents. When Satch pitched for St. Louis against New York, Yankee broadcaster Dizzy Dean recalled for the listening audience a time when they had pitched against each other in a barnstorming exhibition back in Paige's Negro League days many years before.

Dean had led off an inning against Satchel and sliced a short fly over first base that rolled all the way for a triple. As Dean pulled into third base, Paige walked over and said, "Mister, dat's where you is and dat's where you're going to stay", and proceeded to strike out the next three batters.

On September 14 of '51 after Paige struck out Ted Williams by crossing him up, Ted stormed into the dugout and smashed his bat to pieces. Watching this display from the mound, Satchel nearly doubled up with laughter, and said later, "I've never seen anything like that in the big leagues. Ted was sore because I crossed him up. That man must expect to get struck out once in awhile, but if he does that every day, he's going to run out of bats and then he won't have anything to hit with."

Attendance had increased slightly in the first few weeks with the antics supplied by the new Veeck philosophy, but the biggest and most remarkable antic of all was yet to come. Veeck had a truly unique plan to celebrate the 50th anniversaries of both the American League and the Falstaff Brewing Company, which sponsored Browns broadcasts.

It was Sunday, August 19, with the Browns scheduled to host the Tigers in a doubleheader. The 20,299 in attendance could not possibly have imagined what would unfold before their eyes. Upon entering the park amid the festive atmosphere, patrons were given a serving of ice cream and cake, and salt and pepper shakers that looked like miniature Falstaff beer bottles.

Once inside, they observed baseball personality Max Patkin performing his comedy routines wearing a Browns uniform with a large question mark on the back of the jersey. Between games of the doubleheader, Browns broadcaster Buddy Blattner served as master of ceremonies as performers began to appear on the field, including an eight-piece band. Another four-piece band played that was made up of Browns personnel including coach Ed Redys on accordion, Paige on drums, Johnny Berardino on maracas, and Al Widmar on bass fiddle. Also on hand were a clown, several jugglers, and a fleet of antique autos.

Suddenly, a giant birthday cake was wheeled out to home plate, and a character known as "John Falstaff" stepped up to speak a few words. He told the eager crowd that he was going to introduce a "genuine Brownie," and then proceeded to tap on the cake as a tiny, child-like man popped out of it wearing a Browns uniform with the number "1/8" on his back. Eddie Gaedel then ran into the St. Louis dugout as the team's publicity department was sticking to the story that he was "another outstanding player signed by the Browns in their expanded world-wide scouting system."

The ceremonies concluded, and not much more was expected from Gaedel until his moment of notoriety came in the bottom of the first inning of the doubleheader's second game.

As the public address system informed the crowd that Eddie Gaedel would be pinch hitting for Frank Saucier, the 3'7", 65 lb. midget waddled up to home plate swinging three tiny bats. At this point, home plate umpire Ed Hurley and base ump Art Passarella stopped the game to confer. Browns manager Taylor then came out of the dugout and showed the umpires a standard player's contract signed by Gaedel, and they had little choice but to let the game proceed. Tiger pitcher Bob Cain, who had been the loser in Bob Feller's no-hitter seven weeks prior missed the small strike zone with the first two pitches. Catcher Bob Swift then ran out to the mound for a meeting, and they agreed to throw hard fastballs. When play resumed, Cain missed with both, and having walked on four pitches,

EDDIE GAEDEL. *The 3'7" 'Brownie' officially retired with an on-base percentage of 1.000, but this was not his only appearance on a major league ballfield. In the mid-1950s, when Bill Veeck owned the White Sox, he had Gaedel and three other midgets dress in Martian costumes and capture Nellie Fox and Luis Aparicio at second base in yet another stunt.*

Gaedel ran down to first base. He was immediately pinch run for by Jim Delsing as the bases were now loaded.

It was revealed later that Veeck had given Gaedel three orders before his batting appearance:

1. Don't swing under any circumstances
2. Stay as far back in the batter's box as possible
3. Stay in a low crouch

Veeck also said later, "Boy, you should have seen [Tiger pitcher] Cain's face when Gaedel came to the plate. I am sorry there are no pictures of the pitcher's utter amazement." Veeck also chuckled, "He was scared before we put him in the birthday cake, but after we talked to him awhile, he got over it." Veeck admitted that his inspiration to pull off the stunt came from a James Thurber story that had been published in a book called, *The Saturday Evening Post Sport Stories* in 1949.

The notorious pinch hitter in question was something just shy of an overnight sensation. One day he was an office worker and errand boy at *Drover's Daily Journal* in Chicago, residing with his mother at 2801 South Walcott Street in that city, and the next he had 'earned' his place for all time as an entry in the *Baseball Encyclopedia*. It was learned that Gaedel's contract with Veeck would pay him $100 per game, but unfortunately, it ended nearly as quickly as it began.

Later in the afternoon of August 19, American League president Will Harridge issued a statement effectively banning Gaedel from further appearances in official games:

> "The American League office does not approve the contract submitted by the St. Louis American League club for the services of Edward Gaedel on the basis that his participation in American League championship games, in our judgement, is not in the best interest of baseball."

Attempting to keep a straight face, Veeck countered "I have examined the rules of Organized baseball and I can't find a single paragraph which states how tall or small a player must be to be eligible to play." Veeck went on to say that there was a man just over from England who was nine feet three inches tall whom he had been considering inserting in a game as well. Regarding the banishment, Veeck said, "Gaedel's major league career is one of the shortest on record, but I'll bet it won't be forgotten for a long time." Upon hearing Harridge's decision, Gaedel said, presumably with tongue firmly planted in cheek, "Organized baseball should have a commissioner so I can appeal this decision [the office was technically vacant at this time]. "Harridge is ruining my baseball career. This is a conspiracy against short guys. This is a strikeout against the little people."

Gaedel immediately parlayed his newfound notoriety into a stint with a touring rodeo. Two weeks after his baseball career had abruptly ended, he found himself on the road with a traveling show in Cincinnati, where on September 3 he ran afoul of the law. While walking along a downtown street at 3 A.M., two policemen spot-

The jersey that Eddie Gaedel wore in his fabled pinch-hit appearance, on display at the National Baseball Hall of Fame and Museum. Courtesy: National Baseball Hall of Fame and Museum.

ted him, and one called out, "Hey little boy, aren't you out kind of late?" The officer reported that Gaedel then spewed forth "the biggest line of profanity ever heard from one person at us." He was promptly arrested on a charge of disorderly conduct.

Several decades later, Bill Veeck's son, Mike, who incidentally was born in 1951, recalled that Gaedel's "1/8" uniform had been in the Veeck family for many years. He even remembered that the miniature Browns uniform had been worn by Veeck children as a Halloween costume in the years that followed.

New York baseball writer Dan Daniel took to calling the Browns "midgets," but there were still other stunts up Veeck's sleeve. Five days after the pinch-hitting stunt, on August 24, Veeck had what he called "Grandstand Managers" deciding Browns' strategy.

Over one thousand fans were selected and seated in a special section behind the home team's dugout. They were issued large placards that read "Yes" on one side and "No" on the other. Two fans who were appointed coaches held up signs in certain situations asking the appointed fans which strategy to use, such as "bunt" or "hit-and-run." Manager Zack Taylor went along with the gag, as he sat in the stands in civilian clothes in a rocking chair wearing bedroom slippers and reading the paper.

Veeck was even toying with the idea of Browns broadcaster and ex-major league infielder Buddy Blattner playing third base with a walkie-talkie attached to him so that he could broadcast the game from the field while playing ("Here's the pitch . . . and it's a ground ball to me.").

Brilliant sportswriter Red Smith wrote in the *New York Herald-Tribune* in September of Veeck, "Sometimes he oversteps the bounds, but at least he wears his tongue in his cheek and there is no malice in his tomfoolery, but only a skylarking kind of candor that recognizes the inability of the Browns to entertain without slapsticks."

Veeck treated his players very well and was quick to reward them for good performances. After the Browns beat the first-place Indians in Cleveland—no doubt a special occasion to Veeck because he had formerly owned the Indians—he instructed his traveling secretary Bill Durney to take them all to the Halle Brothers store in that city first thing in the morning and treat them each to a fine Fall hat. Two weeks later, the players were given new sweaters from Veeck for knocking the Yankees out of first place on September 11.

The final Browns game of the season was to be in St. Louis on September 30, and the carnival carried on right to the end. Before the game, an exhibition basketball game was staged on a floor set up between second and third base that pitted the Harlem Globetrotters against a team of Browns players, including 'coach' Max Patkin.

With the '51 season now finished, the team had compiled a woeful 52-102 record, good for dead last in the A.L. by a full ten games. The final total on the team's attendance was 293,790, only a slight improvement on their 1950 figure.

Thus brought to a close the six-season managerial career of 53-year-old Zack Taylor. Taylor had been a catcher for Bill Veeck Sr.'s Cubs back in the early 1930s, but when Veeck Jr. took over the Browns, it was obvious to all that he would not be returning as manager in 1952. Since July, Veeck had been seeking a big name to take over as field boss, with Rogers Hornsby's name one of the first to surface. Hornsby was managing Seattle of the Pacific Coast League at the time, and Veeck was also interested in another P.C.L. manager, Joe Gordon of Sacramento. Gordon had played a big part on Veeck's World Championship Indians team in 1948. Veeck had talked to Eddie Stanky about the position, but the Giants were unable to obtain waivers on him to complete the deal, similar to his unsuccessful attempt to acquire Lou Boudreau for the position. Some close to Veeck said he was even considering attempting to lure Joe DiMaggio to accept the position of manager and part-time player/ pinch hitter, which he thought would create considerable interest among St. Louis fans.

By mid-August, Veeck announced that Taylor would be staying on for the remainder of 1951. He added, however, that he had picked his manager for 1952, but the announcement would have to wait as the man was currently employed by another team. That announcement came at a press conference on October 8, at which Hornsby was unveiled as the Browns' new skipper. Veeck signed him to a three-year deal and confirmed that he had been the man he wanted all along. Hornsby wanted to finish his major league career in the city where it began back in 1915, and he had actually managed the Browns in 1933 through '37. Regarding Veeck's theatrical antics, Hornsby said he had no objections to entertainment like fireworks after games, "However, I take my baseball seriously, and if my club is getting beat, I don't want anybody laughing at some clown." Veeck agreed that there would be no more clowns.

The Veeck/Hornsby union may have been doomed from the start as he ultimately lasted only 51 games into the 1952 season. The Browns' tenure in St. Louis would not last that much longer either. One of the earliest accurate predictions of the team's fate came in mid-August of '51 from Bill DeWitt, who had been retained as Browns vice-president. Hugh Trader Jr. of the *Baltimore News-Post* asked him, "What are the chances now, since Veeck moved into St. Louis of the Browns moving to Baltimore?"

DeWitt was said to have replied, "The chances of moving the Browns to Baltimore in two years are good."

History shows that this is indeed what occurred, as Veeck disposed of the team after the 1953 season and the Browns became the Orioles. Veeck would resurface as owner of the Chicago White Sox a few years later, but in his long association with baseball, the 1951 Browns serve as the finest example of the high jinks and color he infused in the game.

7

'SAY HEY' TAKES HARLEM BY STORM

WHEN JACKIE ROBINSON WAS TOURING THROUGH THE SOUTH with a barnstorming team of black players after the 1948 season, a young outfielder joined the team for a short time who managed to catch his eye. The speedy young center fielder so impressed Robinson that he wrote a letter to his Dodger general manager, Branch Rickey, telling him about the promising athlete.

The Brooklyn club failed to act on the advice, and while there was interest from the Boston Braves, it was the New York Giants who managed to secure his name on a contract in the spring of 1950 for a $4,000 bonus and $250 per month salary to play for their Trenton farm team. Little more than a year later after his quick ascent into the Giants' outfield at just-turned 20 years old, many baseball people were convinced of Willie Mays' ability and potential.

Robinson continued to be an admirer of young Mays, saying in late '51 " . . . he's got the tools to become one of the great stars of the game." Al Simmons, one of the outstanding hitters of the 1920s and '30s said in mid-summer: "The best kid I've seen in years . . . look at that stance at the plate . . . look at that poise. He's got every-thing." And his manager and mentor Leo Durocher had the most glowing praise of all shortly after his debut with the team: "There's nobody who's got more power. Mays is gonna be the greatest to lace on a pair of spiked shoes." And, "This is the best-looking rookie I've seen in my 25 years of baseball."

Mays grew up in Fairfield, Alabama, and when his father came home at night from working in the steel mills in Birmingham he often played ball with Willie. Young Mays attended Fairfield In-dustrial High School and not only played baseball but was also a quarterback on the football team. He graduated with a B average and reportedly had the opportunity to attend Tennessee State on a football scholarship, but Willie knew early on that baseball was his game. By 16 years old he was already playing with the Birmingham Black Barons of the Negro Leagues.

Mays spent parts of three seasons ('48, '49, and '50) with the team until the spring of 1950 when the New York Giants purchased him for $10,000. The Birmingham team reportedly needed money after their bus had gone up in flames on a road trip in New York. Willie spent 1950 with Class B Trenton of the Inter-State League, where he hit .353 in 306 at-bats. He was then ticketed for Minne-apolis of the American Association for 1951, just one step away from the big leagues.

The Minneapolis Millers were in Sanford, Florida for Spring Training of '51, when Mays and Leo Durocher met for the first time. It was on March 27 while the Giants were playing an exhibi-tion game in Orlando that Leo drove over to Sanford to see Minne-apolis play Ottawa of the International League in a morning game. The sole purpose of Durocher's trip was to observe Mays, and when he first spotted the 19-year-old youngster he shouted, "Hey, kid, what are you going to show me today?" Millers Manager Tommy Heath told Mays a few weeks later that he didn't think Willie would be with the team all season, and that the Giants were likely to call him up.

WILLIE MAYS. *Young Willie Mays is captured just before his debut with the New York Giants on May 25, 1951.*

Playing with Minneapolis that spring was former longtime Negro Leaguer Ray Dandridge, one of the finer third basemen those leagues ever produced. Sadly, the breaking of the color barrier came a bit too late for Dandridge, who nearing 38 years old, would never get the chance to take the field in a major league game. He did have a positive effect on young Mays, however, befriending him and encouraging him to stay focused and to stay out of trouble.

Mays was set to make his regular-season debut with Minneapolis on April 18 in the night game opener at Columbus as the Millers were defending their 1950 league championship. Playing center field and batting third, Willie had two singles in six at-bats and scored a run in the 14-7 win. Two days later on April 20, still in Columbus, he banged out his first home run with Minneapolis, and also added a double. Mays was getting off to a flying start and was not held hitless until the 13th game of the season, the second game of a doubleheader on April 29 at Indianapolis.

Willie resumed his hot streak in the next game, which was the Millers' home opener at Nicollett Park in Minneapolis on May 1 against Columbus. He witnessed a scene completely new to him this day, with snow being removed from the field before the game. Mays' future Giants teammate Hoyt Wilhelm hurled an 11-0 shutout, and *The Sporting News* made reference to Willie's performance in an article in the May 9 issue entitled "Mays' 12-Tilt Skein Ended, Begins Anew on Birthday," however it contained two factual errors. It read in part:

> "Willie Mays, brilliant young Negro outfielder of the Millers celebrated his 19th birthday in sensational fashion here May 1, banging out a double and two singles in three trips as Minneapolis marked its home opener with an 11-0 triumph over Columbus. Mays also turned in two sensational catches."

Mays would actually turn 20 years old five days later on May 6. The piece was correct in pointing out, however, that in Willie's first 12 games he had gone a very impressive 19-for-51 at the plate. On his actual birthday, Mays had another three-for-five day in the first game of a doubleheader versus Toledo. He went hitless in Game

Two that day, and then began a stretch of seven consecutive multi-hit games in which he went 22-for-30 with four home runs, ten RBI, and 14 runs scored. Through games of May 16, Mays was leading the American Association in batting by a wide margin at .476, and had amazed Millers fans by hitting .607 thus far on the home stand.

In the May 23 issue of *The Sporting News*, Mays was featured in a large cartoon illustration by artist Murray Olderman entitled, "Pounding Path to Polo Grounds." Beside the incredible likeness of the young ballplayer was the proclamation "The Parent Giants Are Already Clucking over Willie's .462 Bat Mark For The First 27 Games." Two issues later, the publication featured a photo of Mays reading the issue and admiring the national coverage he was receiving.

On May 16, Minneapolis went on a road trip that started in nearby St. Paul, and took them to Milwaukee, then Kansas City. Mays again began a string of multi-hit games, the most noteworthy coming on May 19 in Milwaukee as he went four-for-five with a home run and a triple. The Millers had moved on to Kansas City, and the game of May 23 was significant not because Minneapolis won 9-5, or because future Hall of Famer Hoyt Wilhelm relieved for the final 4 2/3 innings to get the victory, but because it marked the final minor-league game that Mays would ever play. He did so in the same park that his counterpart Mickey Mantle would play his home games as a member of the Kansas City Blues later in the '51 season. Willie closed out the minor-league portion of his career in fairly typical fashion, going two-for-five with two RBI.

After the game in Kansas City on the 23rd, the Millers had moved on to Sioux City, Iowa, for an exhibition game when the call came from the Giants. The parent team's center fielder Bobby Thomson had been slumping badly, hitting in the .220s, and Durocher wanted Mays to replace him. Leo had actually considered bringing him up a month before when Clint Hartung and Don Mueller had made miscues in the outfield during a woeful losing streak. When manager Heath told Willie of the promotion, he was extremely reluctant to go. He feared he wouldn't be able to handle major-league pitching and was happy to stay right where he was. Heath had Leo talk to Mays on the telephone at that time, and Durocher was able to convince him that he was ready to make the step.

Mays certainly had nothing left to prove at the minor-league level. He was leading the American Association with a .477 batting average, 98 points higher than his closest competitor, and in the 35 games in which he appeared, he only went hitless twice. He was leaving behind a 16-game hitting streak in progress and many fans who were very sorry to see him go. Late in the season, one writer who covered the American Association speculated that with Mays being such a popular player throughout the circuit, it may have cost A.A. teams a total of $250,000 in gate receipts when he was promoted to New York. In order to assuage the loyal Millers fans, Giants owner Horace Stoneham took out a large ad in the *Minneapolis Sunday Tribune* on May 27 explaining to them that Mays' spectacular record thus far this season warranted his promotion and thanked them for their continued support. The editors of the paper subsequently praised Stoneham for his acknowledgment of the Millers fans.

Mays joined the Giants in Philadelphia on Friday morning, May 25 as the team was finishing up a road trip with a three-game series versus the Phillies. Later he would recall that on the plane flight he carried several bats with him that he placed on the empty seat beside him, and a stewardess asked him if he was Jackie Robinson. The promotion of Mays meant the demotion of Artie Wilson to Ottawa. The 30-year-old Wilson had been Willie's teammate team in 1948. Oscar Ruhl wrote in his *Sporting News* column: "One Birmingham boy's gain was another's loss." Though he had a long career in professional baseball, Wilson's only stop in the major leagues was in 1951. Upon his arrival, Mays was assigned to room on the road with another ex-Negro Leaguer, 32-year-old Monte Irvin. The two had met for the first time the year before when Irvin had come to Birmingham on a fall barnstorming tour. Mays had the opportunity to speak with Stoneham at this time, and the owner warned him that pitchers might test him by throwing at his head.

Willie was unfazed, saying that this had happened from time to time in the Negro Leagues.

Willie was joining a Giants team of which big things were expected, but were floundering in fifth place with a 17-19 record. Durocher immediately inserted him in the starting lineup for that afternoon's game, playing his familiar center field and batting third. Wearing the number "14" on his road gray Giants uniform, he caused a stir in batting practice by hitting several long drives into the left-field stands. As the game got underway, he came up in the top of the first inning and struck out looking against Phillies starter Bubba Church. He went hitless in five at-bats in his debut game, but the Giants came away with an 8-5 win. Though Mays himself might not have believed so at this time, he was to appear in every Giants game for the duration of the '51 season.

The next afternoon, Willie was 0-for-3 with a walk off Phillies ace Robin Roberts, but Larry Jansen's seven-hitter gave the Giants the 2-0 win and finally brought them up to .500 with a record of 19-19. In the final game of the series and the road trip, Sal Maglie beat the Phils 2-0 on a two-hitter, but Mays went hitless again in four trips to the plate.

The team then returned back home and were set to take on the Boston Braves in a night game at the Polo Grounds on Monday, May 28. It would be Willie's first appearance in the Giants' white home uniform, but it was not the first time he had played at the Polo Grounds, having come through previously with Birmingham. He had now gotten off to an 0-for-12 start in his new major league career, and facing lefty Warren Spahn this night held no great promise of breaking the slump. Spahn retired the Giants' first two batters in the bottom of the first inning, and Mays stepped in for his first at-bat with the Giants at home. He then hit a high drive that landed near the left-field roof for the first of what would end up 22 years later as 660 career home runs. Mays went hitless in his other three at-bats that game and his solo home run was the only run the Giants scored in the 4-1 loss.

After two days of rain, the Braves series resumed with a double-header on the last day of May. Willie was 0 for three in the first game won by New York 6-5, and 0 for two in the second game, in which Boston took 6-3. He had to come out of the second game, mid-way through due to painful cramps in both legs.

The next day, June 1, with Pittsburgh in town, Sal Maglie was dominant in an 8-2 win, but Willie looked bad going 0-for-5. Since he had hit the home run, still his only hit since his promotion, he had gone 0-for-13. His worst fears were now being realized. He had sandwiched one home run in between streaks of 0-for-12 and 0-for-13. He was one for 26 now with a batting average of .038.

Maybe it would just be easier to go back to Minneapolis. It was all too much for him as he broke down crying in the locker room after the game. Leo came over and had a fatherly chat with him, reassuring Willie that he was sticking with him as his center fielder. Durocher convinced him to not always try to pull the ball and decided to bat him lower in the order. Willie was also reminded that Jackie Robinson had an 0-for-21 slump after getting off to a quick start.

Mays was now ready to turn the corner on his batting woes as the Giants closed out their series with the Pirates on Saturday, June 2. Batting eighth in the order, he broke through with a triple, a single, two RBIs, and two runs scored as New York pummeled Pittsburgh 14-3. Willie also made a spectacular catch off Ralph Kiner, pulling down a high line drive off the left center field bleacher screen, bumping his head in the process.

He came right back the next day in the first game of a doubleheader against St. Louis and smacked two doubles. Suddenly the game was fun again, as he was convincing himself now that he could indeed hit major league pitching.

It was around this time that Mays first donned his fabled number 24 on the back of his Giants uniform. When reserve outfielder Jack Maguire, who was wearing the number was shipped to the Pirates on June 5, Willie discarded 14 and took over the number that would be his trademark for the rest of his baseball career and beyond. It was also in these early days with the Giants that he began to be referred to as 'Say Hey,' because of his habit of approaching people with these words when he didn't know their names.

On June 6 versus the Reds at the Polo Grounds, Mays knocked out his second home run, a two-run shot off Cincinnati starter Willie Ramsdell. This was the third game of what would turn out to be a ten-game hitting streak for him.

Willie was settling into his new life in New York City. He was living with an older couple on 151st St. who treated him like a son. He still didn't drive a car, preferring to bicycle, and he enjoyed simple things like playing stickball with the kids in the street. He also spent a lot of time with Durocher's son Chris. Leo knew that keeping Willie busy with wholesome activities such as taking Chris to movies and out for ice cream might help to keep the 20-year-old out of trouble in the big city. Durocher wanted to keep him focused on baseball, and young Mays was getting a tremendous education on the game. Willie would sit next to Leo in the dugout, and the skipper would explain the subtle nuances of the game to his favorite young pupil. In addition to Leo, who seemingly thought of every angle tutoring him, other highly intelligent ballplayers, such as Eddie Stanky and Irvin, imparted their considerable knowledge to him as well.

Mays got his first look at Red Sox great Ted Williams in person when Boston came to the Polo Grounds on June 11 to play a benefit exhibition for the National Amputation Foundation. Boston won the contest 5-3, though Mays did hit a home run in the second inning. Two weeks later, Mays got his first look at Fenway Park as the Giants traveled there for another benefit, this time for the Hospitalized Veterans Fund. He was two for two with two runs scored in the exhibition.

Throughout the month of June, Mays was in a groove at the plate, with numerous multi-hit games. He was playing a big part in several victories as the Giants were slowly trying to climb back into the pennant race after their horrible start. On June 18 in St. Louis, Willie hit a two-run home run in the eighth inning to help New York win 5-4.

Four days later in Chicago Mays had struck out three times in the game already, but with the score tied in the tenth inning, he hit a three-run homer off Dutch Leonard that would win the game 9-6. Leonard, at 42, was 22 years older than Mays.

It was during this Giants-Cubs series at Wrigley Field that Chicago manager Frankie Frisch had wired Charlie Grimm, manager of Milwaukee of the American Association and asked him how to pitch to Mays. Grimm wired back that he didn't know because Mays was 16-for-20 the last time they played against him.

Willie was also beginning to receive attention for his defensive abilities. On June 24 in Pittsburgh, Rocky Nelson hit a hard line drive to deep center field. Mays broke hard to his right, but couldn't get his glove in position to catch the ball, so he reached out and caught it with his bare right hand. Later in the summer, in mid-August, he made what was thought to be one of the greatest throws ever seen at the Polo Grounds when he threw out Brooklyn's Billy Cox at home plate with the score tied 1-1. Carl Furillo had hit a fly to normal depth center field and Cox tagged up. Mays caught it, spun completely around, and threw the ball right into catcher Wes Westrum's mitt, who tagged a very surprised Cox easily. Giants secretary Eddie Brannick, who had been around the Polo Grounds since 1908, said it was the greatest play of its kind he had ever seen. The Giants ended up winning the game 3-1, with one of the runs scored by Mays.

By the beginning of July, Mays was back batting in the third spot in the batting order on a regular basis. He began to slump slightly, driving in only three runs in the first ten games, and Durocher moved him down to sixth for awhile. Home runs started to come, and between July 15 and July 22, Mays hit a total of six. On the 22nd versus the Reds he drove in all three Giants runs with two home runs. In all, Mays hit ten home runs in the month of July, exactly half of his season's total with the Giants.

Near the end of July, Willie reached a minor career milestone, which turned into an embarrassing situation. On the 29th while playing the Reds, he stole his first base, then was promptly picked off by Willie Ramsdell. Perhaps Ramsdell had gained a small measure of revenge against Mays after the home run he had hit against him in their previous meeting in early June.

August turned out to be a very eventful month for both Mays and the Giants, as the team would make a move to reduce the seemingly insurmountable lead Brooklyn had built up. Matters weren't helped when the Dodgers completed a three-game sweep over the Giants in Brooklyn on August 9 that put them 11 1/2 games up. Dodger catcher Roy Campanella, who one might surmise would have been supportive of young Mays, actually rode him very hard during the heated matchups between the two teams.

Durocher advised Willie to throw a handful of dirt into Campy's mask the next time he annoyed him while at bat. Some of the other veteran black players around the league also gave Mays a bit of a hard time on occasion. A few, like Campanella who had to start their careers late because of the color barrier seemed to resent the fact that he could walk right in at the age of 20.

It was August 12, having begun the day 13 games out of first place that the Giants began a remarkable 16-game winning streak to vault them back into the race.

In the second game of the doubleheader that day against the Phillies, Mays batted in the cleanup spot for the first time. His spot in the batting order was constantly shifting, ranging at this time anywhere from third to seventh.

The Giants were able to turn the tables on Brooklyn on August 14 through 16 by sweeping three games at the Polo Grounds. The middle game featured the terrific throw by Mays to nail Cox, a key play in the 3-1 win. The next day with the Giants in Philadelphia for a series, Willie was honored by a contingent from nearby Trenton, New Jersey, where he had played in the minors in '50. He was presented with a set of golf clubs, a scroll, and a portrait of himself making a one-handed catch.

It was also this week in the August 15 issue of *The Sporting News* that writer Clay Felker penned an article entitled "Mays Dynamite at Bat, Magnet in Field." In it, legendary sportswriter Grantland Rice referred to him as "the kid everybody likes."

Mays contributed to the 11th straight win of the streak on August 22 when he started a rally in the seventh by singling, then scored on Bobby Thomson's double. The Giants went on to beat the Reds 4-3. Four days later in the second game of a doubleheader with the Cubs, Mays went three for four with two runs scored, including a steal of home in their 14th straight victory. The day before this performance, Willie had the chance to act as one of the guest instructors at a clinic on hitting and fielding sponsored by the New York Journal-American newspaper.

Whether he had begun to wear down from the long season, or pitchers had found a bit of a weakness, Mays's batting tailed off in September. He entered the month hitting in the .290s, but hit at only a .250 clip for the month with just one home run and eight RBI.

He actually lost what would have been an inside-the-park home run on September 3 when he failed to touch third base and was only credited with a double. But despite a slight dropoff in production from earlier in the season, he was still contributing to Giant victories, and of course each victory ultimately was crucial. On September 15 his 20th and final home run of the season helped beat the Cubs and bring New York within five games of first place. On September 29 with the Giants and Dodgers now miraculously tied, Mays manufactured the only run that mattered in their 3-0 win over Boston. He scored the first run of the game in the second inning when he walked, stole second, then third, and scored on a Don Mueller single. After the following day when Brooklyn and the Giants were still tied as the 154 game schedule was complete, Mays would now be participating in only the second playoff in N.L. history.

In the three-game playoff-for-the-ages that vaulted the Giants into their first World Series in 14 years, Mays was basically a non-factor offensively, reaching base only once via walk in his 11 plate appearances. The most lasting memory for him was having a front row seat to the Thomson home run that ended it, watching from the on-deck circle. Mays said later that he was praying that he wouldn't have to come to bat in that situation, and Thomson got him off the hook with his dramatic shot.

Willie would now be capping off his dreamlike rookie season with an appearance in the World Series. Before Game One on October 4, Mays had the distinct thrill of being introduced to his idol Joe DiMaggio during warmups. A photographer took Willie over to meet him and snapped pictures of the two together. Joe was one of the reasons that Willie wanted to be a center fielder, and he had even mimicked his batting stance, having seen it in newsreel footage in theatres back home in Alabama. Photos were also taken of Willie and his fellow rookie Mickey Mantle. When Mays came up for his first World Series at-bat in the top of the first, he made the final out of the inning by flying out to Mantle in right. He did so again to open the sixth, then flew out to DiMaggio in the seventh. Mays gained a bit of revenge by snaring a Mantle fly to end the game, which more importantly, the Giants won 5-1.

Another Mays fly in Mantle's direction in Game Two had nearly tragic implications. Leading off the fifth inning, Willie lofted the ball to right center field that both DiMaggio and Mantle pursued, when Mickey caught his spikes on a drain cover and went down in a heap. Mantle was done until the following spring, and in retrospect, it's remarkable to reflect that Mays, so closely associated with Mantle in the minds of many, would have such an impact on Mickey's career, however unintentional.

In the end, Mantle's team prevailed in the Series in six games, and Mays posted a disappointing performance. In 22 at-bats, he had only four hits, none for extra bases, and only one RBI. As a consolation, Willie virtually doubled his $5,000 salary as the losing team's share of World Series money came to $4,951 per player. Willie and the Giants would have to wait three years to redeem themselves in World Series play, and it would be well worth the wait.

With the 1951 season now in the books, a review of the 20-year-old's offensive statistics indicate that he already was outperforming the average major leaguer. His .274 batting average eclipsed the average N.L. figure of .260, and his .472 slugging percentage was far above the circuit norm of .389. His 20 home runs was tops among all rookies, and 14th best in the entire league despite only having 464 official at-bats. He also drove in 68 runs, and stole seven bases.

It was now the season to honor the top performances of the year, and in early November, *The Sporting News* named Mays as the center fielder on their Major League All-Rookie Team. A week later the publication named him as its National League Rookie of the Year, and the Baseball Writers Association of America followed suit the week after with what was generally recognized as the official Rookie of the Year Award.

Writer Ray Gillespie wrote at the time: "Mays' defensive work bordered on the sensational. Some of his catches in center field were nothing short of miraculous." Larry Doby told a banquet crowd a few weeks later that Mays might well become one of the game's top players, and would learn a lot from Monte Irvin, who was Doby's teammate with the Negro League Newark Eagles.

Mays had intended to go on a barnstorming tour through the South in late October with Irvin, Don Newcombe, Campanella, Hank Thompson, and others. When he arrived back home after the World Series he had received a notice from the draft board of Birmingham to report for a physical within ten days. It soon became evident that Willie was destined for a stint in the military, but the progress he had made in professional baseball in 1951 would provide just a small indication of the heights he would later attain in the game.

8

A CHANGE AT THE TOP

IT WAS AT BASEBALL'S WINTER MEETING in St. Petersberg, Florida in mid-December of 1950 that the 16 major league owners held a vote on whether or not to renew the contract of commissioner Albert "Happy" Chandler. Most were surprised to learn that Chandler subsequently did not receive sufficient support at that meeting, touching off a saga that would take more than 10 months to fully resolve.

The vote for renewal of Chandler's $65,000 per year contract required approval of 12 of the 16 owners. The former minimum of nine votes for election had been changed to twelve a couple of months after the death of baseball's first commissioner, Judge Kenesaw Mountain Landis in November of 1944. It was in April of '45 that Chandler was picked as his successor. Now, less than six years later, Chandler could only garner nine votes among the 16 magnates. One of his more outspoken critics was St. Louis Cardinals owner Fred Saigh, whose main bone of contention appeared to be the television contract that had just been signed. Chandler had agreed to a deal with the Mutual Broadcasting System and Gillette that would

ALBERT "HAPPY" CHANDLER. *Baseball's second commissioner, Albert "Happy" Chandler waves goodbye to baseball in the summer of '51 after an eventful six-year reign.*

pay baseball six million dollars over six years. Saigh was adamant that the rights would be worth more within a couple of years, and went so far as to say he could guarantee he could get more within ten days. He was ultimately proven correct when Gillette resold the rights for four-million dollars per year.

Saigh occasionally referred to Chandler as "the bluegrass jackass", and was thought to be the first to lead the revolt against Chandler. He stated bluntly "I don't think he's a good commissioner, and I'll vote against a renewal of his contract." In attempting to turn other owners against Chandler, he found an ally in Yankee co-owner Dan Topping, who helped to orchestrate the ouster. Webb was quoted as saying, "I don't dislike Chandler. I simply think we could get a better commissioner." Continuing his lack of specifics on the matter, Webb added later, "I did not like Chandler's administration because of the way he handled the job" . . . "Chandler has a lot of abilities, but I found that they were not always directed in the right avenues."

By early January, a four-man screening committee seeking candidates for the position had been created, consisting of Del Webb of the Yankees; Ellis Ryan of Cleveland; Phil Wrigley of the Cubs; and Lou Perini of the Braves. In their search, they used the guidelines that a commissioner should be a prominent person with a spotless reputation who must act as a business executive, public relations man, diplomat, an effective public speaker who is not only a fan of the game, but fluent in its rules and procedures.

The commissioner also directs the player's pension fund, oversees legal issues, counsels team owners, acts as a liaison with the Federal Government, and can represent the game as a goodwill ambassador who places the welfare of the sport above all. Finding a candidate who possessed all of these qualifications would surely be a daunting task.

It was thought at that time that a new election might come as early as February, but it was still not clear if Chandler could still be re-elected. There were many from all walks of the baseball world who supported him. He still appeared to have the support of the nine team representatives who voted to retain him in December.

The nine were believed to be: Horace Stoneham, Giants; Walter O'Malley, Brooklyn; Warren Giles, Cincinnati; Phil Wrigley, Cubs; Tom Yawkey, Red Sox; Art Ehlers, Athletics; Clark Griffith, Washington; Billy Evans, Detroit; and Ellis Ryan, Cleveland. Ryan in particular said he had "been unable to find a single reason why Chandler was not rehired." He went on to say, "The commissioner's job shouldn't depend on a matter of personalities, yet I can't find anything concrete that Chandler has done in his six years in office to cause his dismissal." Gene Kessler, writing for the *Chicago Sun-Times* opined, "When men like Connie Mack, Clark Griffith, Warren Giles, Tom Yawkey, and Walter Briggs openly support Chandler, I am convinced there is no justified reason for ousting the present commissioner."

A few noteworthy ballplayers voiced their support for Chandler as well. Tiger pitcher Dizzy Trout said, "I'm for Chandler, and I know most of the players are. He's a great guy and he's done a lot for the players." Lou Boudreau said, "Chandler has every baseball player in his corner." And no less than Ted Williams agreed, saying, "I know the players are strong for Chandler. (He) has always been good to me."

Minor league officials joined in supporting Chandler also. J. Alvin Gardner, president of the Texas League, went on record as saying that the minor leagues should have a vote in the election of commissioner, as they are impacted greatly by his decisions. He didn't feel Chandler's fate should be in the hands of 16 men, but that each class of minors should have an equal vote. Earl Blue, president of the Sally League, pointed out that the owners do not pay the commissioner's salary. He said that the people who buy the tickets should have a vote in the selection process, and most support Chandler. The majority of fans did in fact support him, and *The Sporting News*, which called for Chandler's re-election in the February 21 issue also editorialized in its March 7 issue that public opinion should be considered because it is their support on which the game depends.

The American Association of College Coaches favored retaining Chandler "because of his tireless and effective efforts to advance the game of baseball." Even entertainer Bing Crosby, part owner of the Pirates said he couldn't understand why Chandler wasn't retained, adding, " He has done a championship public relations job for baseball."

By early February, a few noteworthy individuals had already turned down offers to be considered for the commissioner's job, including Federal Judge Harold R. Medina, Lester Pearson, Canada's Minister of External Affairs, and National Association president George Trautman. Chandler meanwhile, was said to be considering a return to politics.

He had given up a seat in the U.S. Senate back in '45 to take the commissioner's post, and was considering a run for Governor of Kentucky. In the first couple months of '51, Chandler had made several speaking appearances at baseball writers' dinners throughout the country, and addressed his situation at each. In his speech in Chicago on January 14, he defended his time in office, citing the improved standard player contract and the increased security of the pension fund. Chandler believed that keeping the fund strong was one of his principal functions, and proudly stated, "There will no longer be any Hack Wilsons or Grover Cleveland Alexanders wandering the streets penniless." He told a Louisville, Kentucky crowd on January 22: "My cup will be full as long as I can honestly say of my time as commissioner that I never did anything to hurt our great American game."

Two days later at a Cincinnati gathering, he said in his speech that he was proud that baseball had no scandals during his term. Warren Giles, G.M. of the Reds was on hand and was actively and openly campaigning for Chandler to be retained.

At the Boston dinner at the end of January, the commissioner shared his philosophy, saying, "Baseball's responsibility is to the people and players, not the owners. They can police themselves. As long as I'm in baseball, I'm protecting it for the people and players." On the Texas portion of his tour on February 20 he said to an Austin audience, "I've never been told any reason why my contract should not be renewed. It's like fighting in the dark. You can't see your opponent." And the following day in Houston he defied "anyone to prove that any of the decisions I have made as commissioner have been detrimental to the game."

Some felt that Chandler's speech at the New York Baseball Writer's Dinner on February 4 was the perfect forum for him to come out swinging hard at his detractors. He apparently chose not to seize the opportunity, and it was later felt that this unwillingness may have turned a few of his would-be supporters against him.

By mid-February, the screening committee had a list of potential candidates down to four, with a vote set to take place on March 12 in Miami. Chandler, surprisingly, was on the list, along with Frank J. Lausche, governor of Ohio; George Trautman, president of the National Association; and former Postmaster General James Farley. Due to the precarious international situation, the committee eliminated candidates who were involved in federal government.

Still several prominent baseball men were speaking out on Chandler's behalf. Red Sox vice-president Eddie Collins said, "Any man who can survive the sneak punch he got recently won't be counted out the next time they count the votes." Phillies owner Bob Carpenter, believed to have voted against Chandler in December, pledged that if he was the best man on the ballot in March, he would vote for him. Maintaining that he had no quarrel with him, Carpenter said, "The whole affair is developing into a sort of a circus and I am tired of it." 81-year-old Clark Griffith, head of the Senators, called for an end to the secret ballots in the commissioner's election, asking for Chandler's opponents to stand up and reveal themselves. He stated:

> "Last time it was a knife-in-the-back job and a disgrace to baseball. Our every action should be written on the scoreboard, not hidden behind a secret vote. The thinking club owners realize that this game of ours belongs to the people of the United States, not four or five selfish men with petty and personal prejudices against the commissioner."
>
> —*The Sporting News*, March 7, 1951

Representatives from each of the 16 teams gathered on March 12 at the Shoremede Hotel in Miami, Florida to hopefully resolve the commissioner issue.

Chandler arrived, and upon entering, joked to reporters: "The condemned man ate a hearty breakfast and proceeded to the guillotine." As it turned out, the magnates would not be casting ballots for one of four candidates, but decided to simply vote again on whether or not to renew Chandler's contract. Perini, of the screening committee felt it was just too difficult to compile a good list of candidates while Chandler was still in office. It was thought that his resignation, possibly to re-enter politics would help. Some were even questioning if the manner in which the entire process was being handled might scare off good candidates for the position. Cubs owner Wrigley would say later very bluntly: "We made a mess of the commissionership."

As the meeting began at about 11:30 A.M., Chandler left and went to nearby Star Island and waited at the home of Reds owner Powell Crosley Jr. Griffith argued long and loud for Chandler one final time, and Connie Mack also spoke in his defense. Yet little more than an hour later when the votes had been tallied, Chandler had still only received nine votes, with seven dissenters. At about 12:50 P.M., Pirates owner John Galbreath emerged from the meeting and went to Star Island to inform Chandler of the results. The lame duck commissioner returned to the Shoremede about an hour later, and one of his first responses was to reveal that some owners who told him they would vote for him obviously didn't.

He also shared his belief that his secretary Walter Mulbry had been disloyal to him. He approached a group of three N.L. owners and said, "I could run for commissioner against any man in the United States and be elected if the people had the vote." He was also quoted as saying, "This is the only election I've ever lost in which I got the most votes." He also indicated that he would likely step down if his successor was named before his contract officially expired on April 30, 1952. He told the owners, "While I naturally regret the action, I want to make it as easy as possible for baseball to elect a desirable successor and will cooperate to that end to the full-

est extent." He refused to criticize any of his opponents specifically, and made his best attempt to bow out gracefully.

A few weeks later at a dinner in Hollywood on the occasion of
the Pacific Coast League's Opening Game, Chandler said:

> "I have no resentment for any man, living or dead. I had
> the backing of the public, players, umpires, and nine of the ma-
> jor league club owners, but lost my job as commissioner. I have
> not done a single thing to hurt the good name of baseball. If I
> had to do it all over again I wouldn't change a single decision, as
> I always tried to do what I thought was for the best interest of
> baseball while serving as commissioner."
>
> —*L.A. Times*, April, 1951

A couple of weeks later, Chandler did show his bitterness by
saying "Isn't it a strange situation when a majority of the owners
and players in Organized Ball throughout the U.S. want me to stay
in office, but a minority could and did vote me out?"

George Marshall, owner of football's Washington Redskins
was critical of baseball for firing Chandler without giving a reason.
He stated, "Baseball alone has not been hurt. All professional sport
has been hit by this action. It is my feeling that Baseball men owe it
to their public to state exactly why Chandler has been ousted. The
sport has placed a stigma on itself that won't be wiped out by the
mere appointment of a new commissioner to succeed Chandler."

In early April, one unnamed baseball official told the *Chicago Tribune* that they are impatiently waiting for Chandler to resign, and if he doesn't soon, they may demand it.

If this were to occur, the duties of the commissioner would be
taken over by the Executive Council, which is made up of the two
league presidents, plus Tom Yawkey and Warren Giles.

The source did address a few of the factors that may have led
to Chandler's rejection:

> "It was an accumulation of incidents. Chandler seemed to
> take it for granted he had a lifetime job. He even took credit for
> baseball's booming postwar attendance. Many owners were irked

at him for the player's new contract and their pension plan. They were alienated when he insisted on sticking to the five-year ban against players who jumped to the Mexican League in '46. Even after his failure to get the necessary votes [in December] I am confident that had Chandler elected to return to his office in Cincinnati instead of making speeches over the country for his retention that he would have had a better chance of getting a new contract in the recent March convention in Miami Beach, Florida."

—*Chicago Tribune*, April 1951

Regarding the Mexican League situation, when players who had jumped to the outlaw league in 1946 returned a short time later, they were suspended from the majors for five years. Owners had asked Chandler to reinstate them after three years, but he insisted they serve the full five. When these players began to sue to return, the litigation cost baseball $400,000, and Chandler ultimately gave in. This was not forgotten. Chandler was now advising the owners that he would step down as soon as his successor was named, however, if too much time were to pass he would simply leave when it was most advantageous for him to do so. Some of the owners who had voted for Chandler were urging him to stay in office until his contract expired in April of 1952.

Other owners at the same time were even suggesting abolishing the position, with the Executive Council taking permanent control. Galbreath of the Pirates visited with Chandler on April 21 to discuss a severance agreement in order for him to vacate the office early. The search for a successor was well underway, and many names were being bandied about. A.L. president Will Harridge removed his name from consideration, saying he was very happy in his present position.

N.L. president Ford Frick also denied having any interest in the job. The screening committee approached the FBI's J. Edgar Hoover, but he said "Not after what you did to my friend Happy Chandler." Earl Cocke Jr., a World War II veteran and present National Commander of the American Legion was approached despite being only 30 years old. Ex-postmaster General Jim Farley was interested, but was seeking a 15-year contract.

On April 30, Braves owner Perini may have been one of the first to recommend the name of General Douglas MacArthur. In the coming weeks, Chandler himself favored the general as his replacement and said he would step down immediately if MacArthur were elected. Bill Leiser of the *San Francisco Chronicle* reported that Chandler said he would "do everything in my power to see that [MacArthur] is promptly installed, and give him every possible assistance in getting started on the job." MacArthur had attended Yankee, Dodger, and Giant games since being relieved of command by Truman, and Shirley Povich asked in his *Washington Post* column in late May "Could General MacArthur be making a pitch for the commissionership with his frequent attendance at games in the New York area?"

Even the ballplayers expressed concern over the commissioner situation. The Union expected that they would present a proposal whereby they would have input as to who would ultimately be elected. Their primary fear was that when Chandler finally left, he might be replaced by one who does not sympathize with their issues. A.L. player representative Fred Hutchinson of the Tigers had said earlier that they had discussed hiring their own commissioner, and that Chandler was suggested for the job.

Chandler, who had previously served as governor of Kentucky and U.S. Senator was believed to be gearing up for a re-entry into politics. He announced, however, on May 15 at a rally in his hometown of Versailles, Kentucky, that he would not be a candidate for governor of that state. He told the crowd that he would support the candidacy of incumbent Governor Lawrence Weatherby. Meanwhile, Saigh of the Cardinals, a chief nemesis, was complaining that Chandler was making political speeches on baseball's expense account.

In early June, Chandler asked Major League Baseball's attorney John O'Brien to draw up a severance contract that would be presented to the owners before he vacated the position. He was seeking indemnity from lawsuits pending against Organized baseball in which he was named in the event damages were awarded. He stated: "In case the Reserve Clause is ruled illegal, I don't want to wind up penalized by losing my home, my money, and all my worldly belongings." The owners were to meet to vote on whether or not to accept the contract on June 14.

It was at a meeting at New York's Hotel Commodore on that date that the owners voted to officially accept all of the terms of Chandler's resignation agreement. They felt he was deserving of the protection from litigation as he had requested, and his departure date was set for sometime around the All-Star break, about a month away. Chandler had finally decided that it would be in everyone's best interests if he resigned and cleared the way for the election of a new commissioner.

On June 21 at the Carew Tower office in Cincinnati, Chandler made it all official by signing the agreement and announcing that his final day in office would be July 15. With Warren Giles at his side at the press conference, he proclaimed unabashedly "Baseball got to its greatest heights while I was commissioner." He continued, "If I had to do it over again, I would do everything just the same way. I know I did not make any stupid errors. I know I never did anything hurtful to the game." Baseball was now finally ready to turn the page on a chapter that had been dragging on for six months.

By the end of June, Walter O'Malley was urgently stressing the importance of selecting a new commissioner soon in order to present strong leadership to the public as the Senate investigation was soon to begin. O'Malley voiced the opinion that N.L. president Frick would be a qualified candidate. Clark Griffith countered that although he was a friend of Frick, he would not vote for him for the office. He was opposed to electing someone from within the ranks of baseball, as well as from big business, as Yankee co-owner Del Webb suggested. Griffith preferred a strong, prominent national figure. In an editorial in the July 4 issue of *The Sporting News*, three qualifications that a candidate should have were listed: 1. Ability to restore harmony in the ranks of the game, split by the fight over the re-election of Chandler; 2. a thorough knowledge of baseball and its increasingly complex problems; and 3. Experience in public relations.

The publication also endorsed Frick as a strong candidate, as he was back in 1945 until Chandler supporters entered the picture. Within a matter of days, Frick was now reportedly considering accepting the position if elected. He was believed to have the backing of seven N.L. teams, with Giles and the Reds being the only team opposed.

Giles blocked Frick's election as commissioner back in '45 because he thought the successor to Landis should come from outside of baseball, and it was thought that he had not changed his view.

On July 6, Chandler cleaned out his desk and said goodbye to his office staff at CarewTower in Cincinnati. He surrendered the office to Giles as a representative of the Executive Council, and also handed him tickets to the commissioner's box at Crosley Field. Giles immediately gave the tickets back and urged him to use them often.

Chandler said on this occasion:

> "I don't think the owners want a commissioner. If they ever do get around to one, the new man ought to insist on two things I never had: the power to fire the secretary-treasurer of baseball, as well as hire him, and the right over any rule in baseball. Landis had precedence over any rule, but they took it away before they made me commissioner."

Four days later, July 10, Chandler made his last major appearance at the 18th annual All-Star Game held in Detroit. Seated beside him in the commissioner's box was Ty Cobb, who threw out the first pitch. After the game, Chandler was reportedly seen shedding a few tears in the American League dugout.

When the All-Star players themselves had gathered for the game, they were very vocal about their desire to see a new commissioner named soon. They seemed unconcerned over the recent attention focused on the Reserve Clause, or forming a strong union, but felt that having a strong commissioner was in their best interests. They believed that when it came to disputes they may have with owners, or collecting pension benefits, it was he who would protect them.

On his last day in office on July 15, Chandler appeared in Pennsylvania and fulfilled a promise that he had made back in 1946. He was on hand to dedicate a new athletic field known as the Reading Municipal Memorial Stadium, and then went home "to do some fishing in God's country—Kentucky." Within days however, he had resumed work in his law office after not practicing law for 18 years. He appeared in court on July 26 and won an acquittal for seven black men accused of crap shooting. The defendants had maintained that police had raided one of their homes without a search warrant.

Ed McAuley of the *Cleveland News* wrote upon Chandler's departure from office: "The great game of baseball—and I mean baseball from the majors to the corner lots—certainly didn't suffer at the hands of Albert Benjamin Chandler."

Chandler then took his place in the history of the game with an administration marked by two prominent actions—paving the way in early 1947 for Jackie Robinson to begin changing the complexion of major league baseball; and the one-year suspension he imposed upon then Dodgers manager Leo Durocher in '47 for associating with gamblers. Some even speculated that his handling of the Durocher affair may have been a factor in his downfall.

Chandler made one final appearance in connection with baseball on August 6 when he was asked to testify before the Senate subcommittee during their investigation of the game. During his testimony he was critical of the owners, saying, "Some of the owners are new, very new. Some are rich, very rich, and some don't know where first base is."

And also, "Sixteen owners think they own baseball. They don't. The American people own it." In retrospect, he showed that he continued to be progressive and even ahead of his time when he stated that the umpires should work both leagues and be supervised by the commissioner's office rather than the leagues. He also said that it was inconceivable that the country could grow 50 years without the format of the major leagues changing.

"I think baseball should make a survey and re-align the whole thing. The national pastime should be national in character and scope." He added that there were many other cities that could support major league ball, such as Milwaukee, Baltimore, Houston, Dallas, San Francisco, Los Angeles, and Seattle.

Yankees co-owner Webb took one more parting shot at Chandler during the hearings when he snapped: "We wouldn't be in this trouble if we had the proper kind of commissioner. The commissioner should have made a study of Organized Ball, like this committee is doing."

The owners had now planned to vote on a replacement on August 1 in New York. The Screening Committee had sent out questionnaires to the owners to get a feel for the type of leader they thought would be most desirable. Webb wanted a big-business type like Jim Farley; Griffith favored Fred M. Vinson, Chief Justice of the Supreme Court.

Vinson had played college baseball and had remained close to the game throughout the years. Perini still wanted MacArthur, but the General had reportedly told friends that while he might have taken the job years ago, he now felt he was too old. Giles was now saying that he thought Frick would be an acceptable candidate, though he still tended to favor a man from outside the game. He also had doubts that Frick would be supported by A.L. owners because of his longtime association with the N.L.

The election that was to take place on August 1 was put off and rescheduled for August 21 at a joint meeting of A.L. and N.L. owners at the Waldorf-Astoria in New York. At a meeting at that hotel on August 7, the list of potential candidates was thought to be reduced to nine. The known names on the list included Frick, Giles, MacArthur, Dwight Eisenhower, General Maxwell Taylor, and Arch Ward. Eisenhower was heavily involved with military affairs overseas, and was even being considered as a presidential candidate. Taylor was the former superintendent of West Point who was now a deputy chief of staff for Operation and Administration in Washington. Ward was at this time the sports editor of the *Chicago Tribune*, and had helped to create baseball's All-Star Game back in 1933.

FORD FRICK. *New commissioner Ford Frick, center, with A.L. president William Harridge to his right, and Warren Giles, the man who replaced him as N.L. president, to his left. Courtesy: National Baseball Library*

When the group met on August 21, they were set to pull a surprise by electing Air Force General Emmett O'Donnell to the post, but President Truman felt he was too important to the national defense effort and wouldn't permit him to leave. The owners did trim the list of candidates down to five at the meeting, although other names continued to be debated. The final decision now wasn't expected until September 20. The list at this juncture seemed to consist of Frick, Giles, MacArthur, Ohio governor Frank Lausche, and Penn State president Milton Eisenhower, brother of Dwight.

The commissioner's office in Cincinnati was actually being run at this time by acting secretary-treasurer George Denman. The 52-year-old former private detective had served as Chandler's office manager, and had now amazingly been granted by the Executive Council final say on any issue involving the two leagues.

As the September 20 election date drew near, various names had the support of varying sized groups of owners. Though Jim Farley had been thought to be eliminated, the influential Yankee owners were still pushing him. Frick had Red Sox owner Tom Yawkey seemingly act as his campaign manager. Clark Griffith seemed to believe that Giles had the best chance. The Reds general manager continued to decline talking about the job for himself, however, saying that he was mainly concerned with putting together a contending team for next season. J. Edgar Hoover was thought to be able to garner 14 votes, but Truman ordered him to stay with the Federal Government.

The historic meeting of September 20 was held in the Crystal Room of the Palmer House in Chicago. It was a marathon affair that took nine hours before a candidate received the required votes for election, and in the end it came down to Frick and Giles.

The two were hopelessly deadlocked as ballots had to be recast many times in an attempt to break the tie. After the magnates had adjourned for awhile and then returned, Giles had graciously withdrew his name from consideration so that the process could come to a fruitful conclusion. Finally at nearly 10:30 P.M., Frick was unanimously elected, and was to receive a seven-year contract for the $65,000 per year post. It is ironic that, according to Larry MacPhail, Frick would have been elected back in 1945 to succeed Judge Landis had Giles not taken the floor and voiced his opposition to a baseball man getting the position.

The owners were almost universally praised for selecting a candidate who was so completely familiar with how the business of baseball was conducted, as well as the problems it faced. Few were thought to be better equipped than Frick. One of the few who was critical was Chandler, who called it a mistake. The problem, he said, was that Frick represented the owners. He further elaborated,

"The commissioner is elected to protect the players and the public and to see that the owners live up to all the rules and regulations. When they decided to replace me, they should have selected a nationally known man not connected with the game."

It is interesting that decades later, Chandler, Frick, and Giles would be elected to the Baseball Hall of Fame for their contributions as executives.

Upon taking over, Frick accurately predicted big changes ahead for baseball.

"Nothing stands still, and it is the same with baseball. There has been no change in the major league map for 50 years." He foresaw the possibility of expansion and major league teams one day being placed in West Coast cities. In mid-November while speaking in Cleveland, Frick denied that he would be an 'owners commissioner', and added, "I have a triple responsibility. First to the fans. I must watch over the integrity of the game. Second, to the players, whom I must guarantee full rights. Then to the owners."

Stepping up to baseball's highest position, Frick took a moment to reflect on his 17-year tenure as N.L. president. He stated that the accomplishments of which he was most proud were helping to establish the Hall of Fame in Cooperstown, and introducing a pension plan for umpires.

Rewarded for his graciousness and loyalty in the process to elect a commissioner, Giles was offered the position of N.L. president, which he accepted on September 27. He subsequently moved into the same office in Cincinnati that had served as the commissioner's office during Chandler's regime. Giles was replaced as Reds general manager by Gabe Paul, who was beginning a long, distinguished career in that position.

With new leadership at the top, baseball was now set to embark on a decade of unprecedented changes.

9

COLOR IN
THE GAME

IN MID-MAY OF 1951, letters were received by the Cincinnati Reds, the city's police force, and the *Cincinnati Enquirer* newspaper stating that Jackie Robinson would be shot during a Dodgers-Reds game at Crosley Field on May 20. The letters were signed "Three Travelers", and claimed that shots would come from a building beyond the ballpark's center field wall. When Robinson arrived in Cincinnati for the series, he was met by two FBI agents. Jackie recalled that the last time he received death threats was back in 1948.

On the 20th, with the teams set to play a Sunday doubleheader, Pee Wee Reese characteristically showed support for his teammate, saying, "I think we will all wear '42' today and then they will have a shooting gallery." Jackie responded somewhat humorously, "That would be too much trouble for you fellows, because you would have to darken up too."

Black fans were said to have come from as far away as Memphis, Atlanta, and Birmingham to see him play. In the face of what was at the very least a serious distraction, Robinson did not disappoint. He helped win the first game with a prodigious home run,

JACKIE ROBINSON. *Note the batting gloves that Robinson is wearing at Spring Training in Vero Beach, Florida in 1951. They were not commonly used during this era.*

hit ironically to center field, in the direction of the purported potential assassins. The ovation he received was larger than anyone could remember hearing in recent memory at Crosley Field. In the four years since Robinson made his historic debut, very slow but steady progress had been made in the integration of baseball. But an incident such as this showed that a long road had yet to be traveled.

While the door to black players in the major leagues was opening, it was clearly not opened wide, and no festive welcoming committee was anywhere in sight. Through the end of the 1950 season, only twelve black players including Robinson had made an appearance in the majors since the barrier had been broken. Sam Jethroe, the only new player to have been added to the list in that '50 season managed to capture N.L. Rookie of the Year honors.

Conditions in this area were such that the Negro Leagues were still in operation, with the Negro American League consisting of ten franchises. They were: The Baltimore Elite Giants, Birmingham Black Barons, Chicago American Giants, Indianapolis Clowns, Kansas City Monarchs, Memphis Red Sox, New Orleans Eagles, Philadelphia Stars, Raleigh Tigers, and Washington Pilots. The league's annual East-West All-Star Game held at Comiskey Park was a tradition that was still several years away from being deemed obsolete. *The Sporting News* in a January, 1951 issue featured an advertisement for the "Delta Negro Baseball School" in Jackson, Mississippi which boasted of 53 players being placed in the Negro Leagues the previous season. Signs of the segregation mentality were still commonly found, particularly in the deep South.

Milwaukee's American Association team was scheduled to play exhibition games at the University of Texas in mid-March, and were asked not to play their two black players, George Crowe and Len Pearson due to racial problems. Shreveport of the Texas League and Monroe of the Cotton States League had made similar requests for their exhibitions scheduled for early April.

Even Robinson admitted that there were still players and umpires at the major league level who resented him and other black players, not giving them a fair shake. He added, "But I know who they are, and when they give me trouble I have to use that restraint Mr. Rickey taught me to use to turn the other cheek."

Old attitudes die hard, and going into 1951, only five of the 16 major league teams had been progressive enough to allow black players to wear their uniform in an official game. The Senators were said to be on the lookout for black players, but Clark Griffith showed that he might have been holding black prospects to a higher standard when he said, "He will have to be a great one. I am not going to sign a Negro just so I can say I have a representative of that race on the Washington club." He did acknowledge, however, that the time had come for every team to employ black players, but added " . . . the number of eligibles is pitifully small, and I am afraid that the breakup of the Negro League, putting 200 men out of work will not help develop candidates for the majors."

It didn't seem to occur to him that distributing them throughout the organized minor leagues to whatever level they were suited for individually would have solved the problem in short order. In the face of continued criticism on the matter, Griffith finally announced in early May that two had been signed, and were assigned to Erie of the Middle Atlantic League.

One of the Negro League stars of the 1940s, Monte Irvin, was unable to make his major league debut until the age of 30 in 1949. While he was competing in his first World Series in October of 1951, he expressed regret that he didn't get the opportunity to play in the majors ten years before. He said wistfully, "I was 22 then and twice the player I am today. I could run faster and throw harder. My reflexes were sharper, and I could make a lot more use of my power. The only thing riding for me now is that I am smarter."

Two Negro League stars from the 1930s and '40s, Ray Dandridge and Leon Day, were not as fortunate as Irvin, sadly, never getting the call. Dandridge was performing very well with Minneapolis of the American Association 1951, even at the advanced age of 37. His young teammate, Willie Mays, was promoted in May, and many still believe that a quota system prevented Dandridge from joining the Giants with him.

Just as there was an unwritten agreement to not sign black ballplayers before Robinson, the magnates may well have attempted to keep the number to a bare minimum in the several years following. For Day, the timing was just not in his favor. The right handed hurler had several outstanding seasons in the Negro Leagues, most notably with the Newark Eagles, but early in the '51 season he was toiling in obscurity with Winnipeg of the independent Manitoba-Dakota League. In mid-July he signed with Toronto of the International League, and at 34 years old, now finally stood just one step away from the major leagues. Toronto had a working agreement with the St. Louis Browns, and after Veeck took over in July, there would have seemed to have been a possibility of a promotion for Day. The speed Day had possessed however, wasn't what it used to be, and being used by Toronto primarily in relief, he wasn't able to distinguish himself enough to warrant a call-up. But decades later, both Day and Dandridge would be rewarded for their brilliant careers with election to the Baseball Hall of Fame, which thankfully, both lived to see.

On the positive side, considerable progress was made in 1951, with more barriers broken. In his *Sporting News* column of February 7, Oscar Ruhl made special mention of the likelihood that Cleveland would have two "colored" outfielders in the starting lineup this year. It was observed in early June when the Giants filled the bases on hits by Irvin, Mays, and Hank Thompson, that it marked the first time in major league history the bases were loaded with black players. When the Giants used Thompson in the outfield in that fall's World Series, it was the first time in an official game that an all-black outfield played together.

Even certain minor leagues in the South that had seriously frowned upon integrated teams were beginning to change their outlook. It was revealed in late February that black players were set to play with teams in organized baseball in Texas for the first time, with Albuquerque and Lamesa of the West Texas-New Mexico League. In November, Senators scout Joe Cambria signed two Cuban black players for Havana of the Florida International League, a Class B circuit in which blacks had never played. Cambria pointed out that Southern cities and their fans were now taking a more liberal view of black ballplayers in organized baseball in recent years. He elaborated: "Jackie Robinson was permitted to play in Atlanta and other Southern cities where there were supposed to be racial barriers and there were no incidents, and those teams of touring colored players which Robinson and Roy Campanella led through the South this fall were given warm receptions." With regard to Robinson's postseason barnstorming tour through the South, Jackie was quoted in a *Sporting News* column by Frank Finch in the November 21 issue:

> "There was one very encouraging aspect to the tour through the South, and that was the amazing overall change in attitude there towards Negro players. The reaction now compared to when I first played down there in 1947 is unbelievable." " . . . It just goes to show what can happen in America."

North of the border, a managerial hiring occurred on March 17 that was far ahead of its time. Farnham (Quebec) of the Provincial League announced that Sam Bankhead, brother of Brooklyn pitcher Dan Bankhead was named the first black manager in organized baseball. The shortstop/second baseman managed the Homestead Grays to pennants in '49 and '50, and would also be a player-manager for Farnham. Though the first black major league manager was still over two decades away, this didn't prevent Jackie Robinson from pondering the possibility. He had revealed in January that one of his great ambitions was to become a big-league manager, and added:

> "Don't think I haven't dreamed about it. Of course, I'm not kidding myself and I know the possibilities are slim right now. The time still isn't ripe for it and the time may never come, at least for me. But I know that someone in my race will have that honor, and how I would love to be that person nobody will ever know."

Still more barriers were crossed as the Philadelphia Athletics hired future Hall of Famer and Negro League legendary third baseman Judy Johnson as a scout in January.

And in July, a young umpire named Emmett Ashford took a two-month leave of absence from his job with the U.S. Postal Service to become the first black umpire in Organized baseball in the 20th century. He made his debut on July 7 in the Southwest International League in a game between Yuma and Mexicali. Fifteen years later in April of 1966, he would in a sense become the 'Jackie Robinson of umpires', beginning a distinguished career in the American League. The winds of change were even blowing in sportswriting circles as the BBWAA was for the first time seriously considering admitting black writers to their circle.

On major league playing fields, several black players were giving a good indication of their collective future in the game. Not surprisingly, Jackie was leading the way, and as late as the first days of June, he was maintaining a batting average in the low .400s. Brooklyn manager Chuck Dressen raved of Robinson at the end of the season, "He's positively the greatest player I've ever managed or coached."

In early October, the Boys Athletic League announced that a nationwide poll of youth organizations had determined that Robinson and Joe DiMaggio were regarded as the country's favorite present-day athletes.

Larry Doby, who of course was a pioneer in integration as well, was being honored for his efforts and accomplishments. At a Cleveland baseball dinner on January 22, the title of that city's "Baseball Man of the Year" was bestowed upon him. He delivered a very moving acceptance speech, thanking among many others, Bill Veeck, who himself had been an active proponent of integration in the game. Doby was also honored with a ceremony at "Larry Doby Day" at no less than hallowed Yankee Stadium on June 23 by a group from his hometown in Paterson, New Jersey. A man who couldn't have worn a major league uniform in Yankee Stadium five years prior had certainly come a long way.

Minnie Minoso was fast distinguishing himself as one of the most exciting players in the American League in his first full season

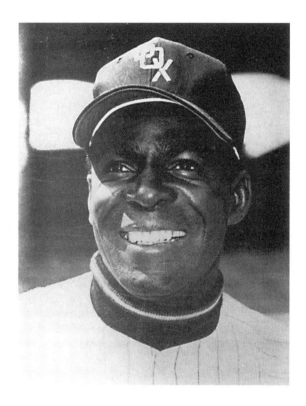

MINNIE MINOSO. *Many felt "The Cuban Comet" should have been the official A.L. Rookie of the Year for 1951.*

in '51. He ended up second in the batting race at .326 and led the circuit in both stolen bases and triples. Veeck said of him in June: "I don't believe there's a player in the game today who can give you the thrill that Minoso can. I love to watch him play." On September 23 at Comiskey Park, the White Sox celebrated "Minnie Minoso Day." In November, *The Sporting News* named Minoso and Willie Mays Rookies of the Year in their respective leagues. Minoso received 122 votes to beat out Gil McDougald with 100, yet in the official Rookie of the Year voting conducted by the BBWAA, McDougald narrowly edged Minnie 13 to 11. In the A.L. MVP voting, which was won by Berra, many questioned how Minoso could get 120 points, compared to only 63 for McDougald, then lose the Rookie of the Year vote to the Yankee infielder. Mays winning in the N.L. marked the fourth time in the five-year history of the award that a black player captured the honor in that league.

The N.L. MVP Award was captured by Roy Campanella, and the fact that one voter left him off his ballot entirely prompted Jack Orr of the *New York Daily Compass* to question, "was the voter blinded by Roy's color?" Regardless of his somewhat glaring omission, it was observed that along with Campy's first-place finish, Monte Irvin ranked third, and Robinson sixth.

Veeck had hired Rogers Hornsby in October of '51 to manage his Browns for the following season. *Jet Magazine* wrote shortly after that despite Hornsby's one-time opposition to blacks in the majors, he would have more on his team than any other within two years.

Truly, the door to so many talented and deserving players was beginning to open ever wider. The pioneers of the late 1940s and early '50s were paving the way for the arrival of future greats Hank Aaron, Ernie Banks, and so many others who made the game better, more exciting, and more complete.

10

NECROLOGY: BASEBALL MOURNS

THE SPORT OF BASEBALL is capable of eliciting a fairly wide range of emotions, including sheer joy or extreme sadness. One of the most somber moments the game's followers experience is learning of the passing of an old-time legend of the past. At least four such incidents occurred in the baseball world during 1951.

On Easter night, March 25, one of the game's most accomplished second basemen, Eddie Collins passed away in Boston. Collins had suffered a cerebral hemorrhage the previous August, but recovered enough to resume his duties as Red Sox vice-president on a part-time basis. His passing was somewhat unexpected as he had maintained a fairly high degree of visibility to the baseball public in the last couple of months of his life. On February 2, the Boston chapter of the BBWAA presented him with the Paul Shannon Trophy for outstanding achievement and services meritorious to baseball. The following day he attended the National League's 75th anniversary celebration in New York, along with several fellow

Hall of Famers. Collins had also been an outspoken critic at the time of those owners who were attempting to remove Commissioner Chandler from office.

For several years he had been affiliated with the Association of Pro Ballplayers, a charitable organization that aided old-time players in need. At the time of his death he was president-emeritus and chief spokesman of the organization, which was regarded as one of the more worthy causes in the game. An editorial in the *Sporting News* published shortly after his death stated:

> "Collins was an exemplar of all that is fine in baseball—a hustling performer who always gave his best, a clean-living gentleman of high ideals, a zealous apostle of the diamond sport, and a friend of the aged, ill, and indigent ex-players."

It was recalled that Collins had passed on an opportunity near the end of his career as an active player that likely would have altered the duration of his baseball life. After Yankee manager Miller Huggins passed away in 1929, Collins turned down an offer to replace him. It seems that Connie Mack had promised Collins that he would be his successor as Athletics manager when Mack retired. When it became clear that Mack was in no rush to retire, Collins accepted the job as Red Sox general manager shortly after Tom Yawkey bought the team in 1933. He went on in that capacity to play a big role in the signing of Bobby Doerr and Ted Williams later in the decade.

The lofty credentials accumulated in his 25-season playing career, which concluded in 1930, include a .333 batting average; 3313 hits; 743 stolen bases, which was second to only Ty Cobb; and six trips to the World Series. His 14 Series stolen bases still ranks as a fall classic record. Collins was one of the early electees of the Baseball Hall of Fame, receiving the honor in 1939, and he was on hand to be enshrined that summer as the institution opened its doors for the first time. His image will forever live in the famous group photograph taken that day, featuring immortals such as Babe Ruth, Walter Johnson, Honus Wagner, Cy Young, and a select few others.

Before the All-Star Game of 1951 was played at Briggs Stadium on July 10, a moment of silence was held in memory of one of the city's beloved baseball figures. Harry Heilmann, one of the greatest right-handed hitters of all time and a longtime Tiger broadcaster, passed away from lung cancer the day before at nearby Henry Ford Hospital. He had been stricken in mid-March during Spring Training and rushed to the hospital in Lakeland, Florida, where he was diagnosed with the disease.

Heilmann had built up a stunning resume as a hitter in the 1920s, winning A.L. batting titles in Detroit in 1921, '23, '25, and '27. His high of .403 in '23 helped to contribute to a mark that had settled at a remarkable .342 upon his retirement in 1932.

Ted Williams, for one, was heartbroken to learn of Heilmann's passing. He reflected at the time:

> "Whenever I was in a slump, I always loved to hear Harry's voice on the phone, inviting me over for a talk. After the kind words he would express to me and the valuable advice he was so willing to give me, I'd always leave him and he'd say 'Humph, Four hundred isn't so hard to hit!' "

Heilmann had narrowly missed election to the Hall of Fame in early 1951 by just 17 votes, but he sailed in posthumously in '52 as the leading vote-getter.

The man who is generally regarded as the greatest umpire baseball has seen was taken from the game two months later. Bill Klem, who served as an N.L. ump from 1905 through 1940 died of heart and kidney trouble in Miami, Florida, on September 16.

Physically unimposing at 5'7 1/2" and 157 lbs., Klem made his mark in a rough-and-tumble era and in the process helped to raise the stature and dignity of the profession. He also is creditd with pioneering the use of arm signals to indicate his calls.

When the flamboyant, colorful man in blue known as "The Old Arbitrator" finally stepped down as an active umpire, he reigned as the chief of staff until his death. He and A.L. counterpart Tommy Connolly would fittingly become the first umpires selected to be in the Baseball Hall of Fame, being so honored in 1953.

It had been a full 30 years since the dreadful 'Black Sox Scandal' had surfaced and rocked the baseball world, yet the name of one of its most famous alleged participants still surfaced from time to time. "Shoeless" Joe Jackson was still a figure capable of evoking strong opinions from longtime observers of the game.

The 63-year-old Jackson was preparing for a moment in the national spotlight as he was scheduled to appear on Ed Sullivan's "Toast of the Town" on December 16.

Sadly, the appearance was never made as Jackson succumbed to a fatal heart attack a week-and-a-half prior on December 5 in his hometown of Greenville, South Carolina. Hundreds of mourners, including several prominent baseball men attended his funeral on December 9.

In September he had been honored with election into the newly created Cleveland Indians Hall of Fame. In his scheduled appearance with Sullivan, Jackson was to be presented with a gold clock to commemorate the honor. Back in February when the National League held its 75th anniversary gathering, writer Ward Morehouse commented on how many of the notable figures present brought up Jackson's name and recalled him fondly. He wrote: "Perhaps I should have obeyed an impulse to bring old Joe up from Greenville on my own, and just had him poke his big gray head into the doorway. He would have received an ovation, Black Sox or no Black Sox." A few weeks later on February 21, the South Carolina House of Representatives introduced a resolution aimed at reinstating Jackson as a member in good standing of organized baseball, and intended to present it to the commissioner. Jackson himself continued to maintain his innocence at this time, and stated "The supreme being is my judge, and not any man in baseball."

A half-century later, there are still those who feel that Jackson's lifetime ban from baseball should be lifted now that he is deceased, and that a place should be made for him in Cooperstown.

11

ONE HOT JULY; ONE SCORCHING SEPTEMBER DAY

ON OCCASION, WHEN A BALLPLAYER RISES so far above what is generally expected of him, observers may go so far as to wonder if he has struck some type of 'deal with the devil'.

Catching lightning in a bottle, he ever so briefly experiences a level known only to the very elite of the game. In reviewing the performance of journeyman outfielder Clyde Vollmer of the Boston Red Sox during July of 1951, one is hard-pressed to form a logical, rational explanation for his consistent productivity in clutch situations.

Vollmer had hit a home run in his first major league at-bat with Cincinnati back in 1942, but had done little since then to distinguish himself. The Red Sox had acquired him from Washington in May of 1950 to serve as a backup outfielder. No one could have foreseen the contributions the fairly anonymous player would make when the calendar read "July, 1951."

As the New York Yankees came in to Boston for a three-game series beginning on July 6, the name Clyde Vollmer was not high on the list of hitters Yankee pitchers were concerned about facing. In the series opener, Boston was clinging to a slim 3-2 lead in the bottom of the sixth inning. With two runners on, Vollmer tripled high off the left-center field wall to score two, then came in to score himself a moment later for what would be a 6-2 victory. The following day, the Red Sox held a 2-0 lead when Vollmer crushed a grand slam which accounted for the winning runs in a game that ended 10-4.

In the series finale on July 8, Vic Raschi was holding a 3-2 lead when Clyde hit a two-run home run and Boston went on to win 6-3. After the sweep, a puzzled Casey Stengel asked, "Where did they find THAT guy? Vollmer isn't that good a hitter, not the guy I used to know. He's not going to keep hitting us like that, I'll tell you that." Luckily for Yankee pitchers, Boston was not scheduled to play New York again in July.

After a three-day layoff for the All-Star break, Vollmer picked up where he left off, now in Chicago. In the first game of a twi-night doubleheader on July 12, he hit a two-run homer off Joe Dobson in the seventh inning to help Boston win 3-2. In the night cap he hit a sacrifice fly in the 16th inning to win 5-4. The next night, Friday the 13th, Vollmer hit a home run in the fourth inning off lefty Billy Pierce to give the Red Sox a 2-0 lead. Chicago came back to tie, and at the end of 18 innings it was still 2-2. In the 19th with runners on first and second, Vollmer hit a single to score one and another eventually scored. Chicago, however, did come back to win 5-4. The next day, Vollmer hit a single in the ninth to beat Chicago 3-2.

Boston's road trip moved on to St. Louis, then Cleveland, as he continued to hit. In Boston's 4-3 win over the Indians on July 18, Vollmer hit a solo homer early in the game, and scored what would be the winning run in the sixth inning. The next day, though Boston fell to Cleveland 5-4 in the eleventh inning, Clyde did his part with two home runs and three RBI. His 18-game hitting streak was finally snapped on July 20 in Detroit, but he resumed the next

CLYDE VOLLMER. *Vollmer went on such a hot streak in the summer o f 1951, he even appeared in an ad endorsing Louisville Slugger baseball bats. Courtesy: Sports Museum of New England*

day going 3-for-4 with a home run, a double, and four RBIs. The Red Sox 6-3 win enabled them to increase their hold on first place from percentage points to a half-game. Vollmer had now hit nine home runs in his past 18 games. When they ended their western road trip on July 22, Clyde had accumulated 18 RBI on the jaunt, only four less than the rest of the team combined.

With the Red Sox back in Boston, Vollmer had his greatest, most clutch day of all against the White Sox on July 26. In the first inning of what was destined to be a high-scoring affair, he hit a two-run home run to break a 3-3 tie. In the fifth frame he hit another homer, this time breaking a 7-7 tie. An inning later he slugged a three-run blast to break a 10-10 tie and win the game by a score of 13-10. Not quite finished with his heroic batting feats, Vollmer had another big game two days later in a 16-inning marathon against Cleveland. He singled in the bottom of the 15th inning to tie the score at three, but the Indians went ahead again by one run in the top of the 16th. Then with Bob Feller on in relief in the bottom of the inning, Vollmer incredibly hit a grand slam to win the game.

As the month was coming to a close, the 'sudden superstar' had hit 12 home runs and collected 35 RBI in the 20 games between July 6 and July 30. He had created such attention for himself in the sports world, that in the July voting for the annual Ray Hickok Professional Athlete of the Year Award, he received 21 votes, good for third place. He was even being featured in ads for Louisville Slugger baseball bats in early August. While many attempted to speculate on reasons for his torrid pace, Vollmer himself simply said, "I guess I'm meeting the ball better."

By early August, the nearly magical powers that Clyde Vollmer seemed to possess began to subside.

Many weeks later, on September 14, Vollmer was playing right field as the Red Sox were hosting the St. Louis Browns at Fenway Park. In the starting lineup for the Browns that afternoon was a young left fielder named Bob Nieman, who was making his major league debut. The 24-year-old Nieman had just won the Texas League batting title while playing for Oklahoma City.

In his first at-bat of the game, Nieman hit a 2-1 pitch from Marty McDermott into the left center field screen for a home run,

BOB NIEMAN.
Nieman's auspicious debut in 1951 included a batting feat that has yet to be topped. Courtesy: Associated Press.

to add his name to a short list of players to have done so in their first big-league at-bat. The next time he stepped up to the plate a couple of innings later, he created a list all his own by hitting a 3-2 pitch, again off McDermott, over the left field screen and onto Landsdowne Street. To this day, Nieman remains the only major leaguer to have homered in his first two plate appearances.

There is a bit more of a connection between Nieman and Vollmer than merely sharing the distinction of hitting a home run in their first at-bats. Both were Cincinnati natives who attended Reds games at Crosley Field as youngsters. In discussing his record feat after the two-homer game, Nieman even made reference to Vollmer. He mentioned that he had tried out with the Reds in 1947, and added, "Clyde Vollmer was with them at the time, but he wouldn't remember me."

Vollmer would certainly remember him after September 14, 1951.

12

CHIEF LEADS NO-HIT PARADE

SCANNING THE OFFICIAL LIST OF ALL NO-HITTERS to ever be hurled in the history of major league baseball reveals a wide range of stature within the game amongst those who have accomplished the feat. It has been done by several who would rank with the greatest pitchers to have ever pitched a ball; others who have had noteworthy careers; and still others who, save for their one moment in the sun, went on to relatively nondescript stints in the big leagues. The four no-hitters thrown in the majors in 1951 serve as a microcosm of this general concept.

The first hitless gem of the campaign was authored by a pitcher who clearly occupies the latter category. Twenty-nine-year-old southpaw Cliff Chambers, toiling for the lowly Pittsburgh Pirates was set to attempt to start the second game of a doubleheader against the Braves in Boston on May 6. Raising doubts regarding his potential effectiveness was the fact that he had spent the previous four days in bed with the flu. Opposing Chambers on the hill for Boston was George Estock, who was making his major league debut.

By the time the Braves' Luis Olmo flied out to George Metkovich in shallow center field to end the game, Chambers had walked a total of eight batters, but more importantly, he had allowed no hits in the 3-0 victory. He became the first Pirate to throw a no-hitter since Nick Maddox back in 1907, and the first left hander to hurl one since Clyde Shoun in 1944. One note on opposing pitcher Estock—1951 turned out to be his only season in the majors, and this particular game was the only one he would start, with all other appearances coming in relief.

Chambers received a letter of congratulations for his achievement from Commissioner Chandler, and before the Pirates game on May 11 he was presented with a wrist watch by Pittsburgh baseball writers. In his follow-up starting assignment, Chandler lasted only two innings before leaving the game with a sore arm. As it would turn out, the no-hitter was his final victory in a Pirates uniform. Chambers was traded to the St. Louis Cardinals on June 15 of that season. By the conclusion of his major league career in 1953, he had compiled a lifetime record of 48-53.

The next masterpiece of 1951 was turned in by a man who was no stranger to such performances. Cleveland fireballer Bob Feller had first added a no-hit game to his resume on Opening Day, April 16, 1940, and duplicated it on April 30, 1946. He also had ten one-hitters to his credit and was looking to tie Cy young and Larry Corcoran of the 1880s as the only pitchers with three no-hitters in the majors. The likelihood of such a possibility was actually broached by a couple of diverse sources. Feller's wife, Virginia, would later relay the story of her premonition of the event. She said, "We were lying on the sand down in Florida one day last winter, when I suddenly said to Bob 'I have the funniest feeling you're going to pitch another no-hit game this year'."

When Feller entered the Indians dressing room at noon on July 1 to prepare for that day's start against Detroit, rookie Milt Neilson asked him "Did you see the morning paper? It says you'll have to pitch a no-hitter today to keep from being the first pitcher on our club to allow 100 hits. You've got 99 now." Of course, at the conclusion of that day's game, Feller had still given up 99 hits for the season.

Tiger outfielder Vic Wertz came to bat with two out in the ninth and lined the first pitch hard down the first base line, foul by just inches. A month before, Wertz had broken up Indian Bob Lemon's perfect game in the eighth inning with a home run. It was Lemon who had pitched the A.L.'s last no-hitter almost exactly three years prior on June 30, 1948.

Finally, with a 3-2 count on Wertz, Feller threw a slider that caught the outer edge of the plate as umpire Charley Berry called strike three. There were many in attendance who actually forgot that the Tigers hadn't gotten a safety due to the fact that they had pushed across a run earlier in the game, and homeplate ump Berry was among them.

Berry finally realized it when he got back to the dressing room and fellow umpire Ed Hurley asked him how many no-hitters he had worked. Bob Cain, the losing pitcher, had bad luck against the Indians, as he had been on the losing end of a Lemon one-hitter the month before.

Feller was hailed after as 'the greatest pitcher of our generation', and 83-year-old Young, whose record he had tied, had listened to the game on the radio. When asked for a quote shortly after, old Cy said, "Walter Johnson was tops, but Bobby Feller isn't too far away."

Eleven days later on July 12, Feller was set to oppose the Yankees Allie Reynolds in Cleveland in the first game back after the All-Star break. The contest shaped up to be quite a pitchers duel, with the first run of the game coming on Gene Woodling's solo home run in the top of the seventh inning. After the bottom half of the inning, Reynolds flouted tradition when he returned to the Yankee bench and said to fellow pitcher Eddie Lopat, "Think I'll pitch a no-hitter Eddie?" Lopat merely gulped. Reynolds scoffed at superstition and was smiling at the end of the 1-0 win with the no-hitter safely in the books. The Creek Indian from Oklahoma had dominated the Indians from Cleveland and rendered Bob Feller, with his four-hitter the loser.

ALLIE REYNOLDS. *Reynolds starred in football at Oklahoma A & M and had an offer to play for New York's football Giants, but it was on the pitcher's mound that he distinguished himself.*

By the time Reynolds' career concluded a few years later, he had compiled a very noteworthy pitching resume; 182 big-league victories; a two-time strikeout and shutout leader; contributions to six World Series winning teams. But it was the last regular season game he pitched in 1951 on September 28 that really placed him in exclusive company and stands as his most unusual distinction.

That afternoon, the Yankees were hosting the rival Boston Red Sox in a doubleheader, and needed one win to clinch a tie for the pennant. In this truly clutch situation, Reynolds came through in a more impressive fashion than anyone had a right to expect, and earned a place in history in the process. When an imposing hitter such as Ted Williams strode to the plate with two out in the ninth inning, Reynolds was remarkably on the verge of duplicating his no-hit feat from two-and-a-half months prior. There were however, anxious moments right to the end.

With one strike on him, Williams hit a towering foul ball that Yogi Berra dropped as fans gasped. With an error charged to Yogi, one of baseball's most dangerous batters had new life. Luckily, Ted fouled off the next pitch as well, but this time Berra settled under it and made no mistake about it. On "American Indian Day" the 32-year-old native American had helped his team clinch a tie for the pennant by doing what only Johnny VanderMeer had done before him—pitched two no-hitters in one season.

In an odd coincidence, Yankee co-owner Del Webb had attended Reynolds' first no-hitter in Cleveland in July, and did not attend another Yankee game until his second on September 28.

Two days later before the Yankees' final game of the season, Reynolds was presented at home plate with the pitching rubber from Yankee Stadium that he had pitched off during his second gem. It was signed by his Yankee teammates as well as his victims, the Red Sox.

13

YANKEE CLIPPER SAILS AWAY

SINCE HIS FIRST APPEARANCE with the team 15 years prior, he had been elevated to almost god-like status; an image cultivated not only by his actual performance, but by the way he carried himself both on and off the playing field. He was the ultimate winner and a true champion; a man who had been on the side of the World Series winners eight times in the 12 years he had played, and had been a key figure—many times THE key figure —each and every year.

Now, as 1951 began, Joe DiMaggio's future as a baseball player was a subject that was to be cause for speculation throughout the entire calendar year.

Yankee management had mailed DiMaggio his contract in mid-January for the '51 season, and the figure was believed to be the same $100,000 that he had received the previous two years. A few other items regarding Joe had shown up in newspapers around this time. He was said to have turned down $5,000 to appear on the Milton Berle television program because he felt he might look silly and undignified in a proposed comedy sketch. It was on January 11 that his San Francisco home was damaged slightly by a tornado, and he was also rumored to be dating his ex-wife Dorothy, with the possibility of remarrying. Yankees owner Dan Topping and general manager George Weiss called Joe at his mother's home in San Francisco in early February to discuss his contract. He had been spending a great deal of time there over the winter with his mother, who was battling cancer. DiMaggio verbally agreed to terms at this time, and would be dropping the signed contract in the mail. The $100,000 figure was a far cry from the $7,000 he had been paid back in his rookie season of 1936. Joe reported that he weighed about 200 pounds and had been golfing regularly with his brother Dom. He was generally shooting about 102, beating Dom fairly often at a quarter per round. Joe also said that his shoulder would pop out now and then, but the left knee that troubled him during the World Series the previous fall was fine. Leo Durocher had run into him in late January and reported, "Joe looks rested, in great physical condition, and should follow up with another impressive year."

Joe had come back with a very DiMaggio-like season in 1950 after suffering through an injury-plagued year in '49. He had been talked out of retiring after that year, but now the talk was surfacing again. In mid-January, Yankees backup catcher Charlie Silvera was asked if he thought DiMaggio would retire, and he replied, "Every night before I go to bed I pray he won't."

In mid-February, Joe told reporter Milton Gross that he had forgotten about the heel that had troubled him, and reiterated that the pain in his left knee was gone. As far as retirement rumors, he said, "I'm going as far as my body will carry. I'll know when to quit. Nobody will have to remind me. I won't be a drag on the club."

Joe arrived at training camp in Phoenix by car on the last day of February, and joined the rest of the position players for their first workout as a full squad on March 1. During that first week, Joe allowed veteran New York sportswriter Dan Daniel and two other reporters into his room at the Adams Hotel for a brief interview. While he munched on cashews, he told the scribes, "This might be my last year. I would like to have a good year and then hang them up."

When asked if he might consider managing, he indicated that he had enough headaches managing himself to be able to handle an

JOE DIMAGGIO. *The Yankee Clipper's popularity around the league was such that White Sox General Manager Frank Lane said in September of '51 that he dreaded the day that Joe retired because he drew as many as 5,000 extra fans.*

entire team, and planned to have no connection with baseball after his playing days were through. "I have a lot of propositions, and I am in no hurry to make a decision. After all, I have another season before me."

DiMaggio admitted that he could likely go on playing for a few more years, but had no intention of fading out gradually. When his brother Dom was asked at the Red Sox training camp about Joe's possible retirement, he responded candidly, "I wouldn't doubt it. Joe often said when he couldn't be head man on the Yankees, he would wrap it up. He always cited the anti-climax to Babe Ruth's brilliant career and his stumbling exit." Yank G.M. Weiss said he hoped Joe would change his mind at the end of the season, but as a precaution, efforts were being stepped up to convert aspiring rookie Mickey Mantle from shortstop to the outfield.

DiMaggio saw his first Spring Training action against major league competition on March 10 in Tucson versus the Cleveland Indians. Joe was sent up to take his swings as a pinch hitter for pitcher Bob Porterfield in the fourth inning and harmlessly popped out.

The next day, however, he pinch hit for Eddie Lopat against the Indians again, and this time hit a home run. For the first several days, Joe was breaking in slow by handling pinch-hitting duties. At the same time in the Los Angeles area, his ten-year-old son, Joe Jr. was trying out as the center fielder on the Black Fox Military Academy team.

The Yankees were scheduled to engage in a week-and-a-half long tour of California beginning on March 16 in Hollywood. The team was honored at the Phoenix Country Club on the 14th before they were to depart, but Joe was not in attendance as he had flown ahead to meet his wife and son. His wife was in attendance at every Yankee exhibition held in the L.A. area, further fueling rumors of a reconciliation. In an interesting sidenote, Marilyn Monroe had just served as hostess at the annual Kiwanis Club benefit baseball game between major leaguers and P.C.L stars in Hollywood a few days before Joe's arrival. She was featured in publicity stills posed with various players, wearing a baseball cap and glove.

As the tour got underway, young Mantle seemed to be stealing the show. He was one of the most talked-about players on the Yankees, as writers in the various cities wanted to know all about him. In the March 17 exhibition at L.A.'s Wrigley Field he hit an amazing home run to deep center field against the minor league Angels, while DiMaggio went 0-for-2 and left the game after his second at-bat. Joe pleased the crowd the next day against the same team, however, as he hit a home run. On the 20th, New York played the White Sox in Stengel's hometown of Glendale, California, in what was billed as "Casey Stengel Day." Joe had an uneventful 0-for-3 day. His batting progress thus far this Spring was slow, and through games of March 20 he had only two hits, though both were home runs, in 18 plate appearances. Neither Joe nor Stengel appeared overly concerned.

On the way up the coast, the Yankees had a stop in Sacramento, and Joe, Phil Rizzuto, and Joe Page dropped in on the California legislature. They each spoke a few words, and when DiMaggio told the politicians that some of them appeared in better shape than some ball players he had seen that spring, he received a round of applause. The next day, the Yankees were in San Francisco to take on Joe's former minor league team, the Seals.

When he came out and began to take batting practice, many fans in the stands yelled at reporters gathered around the cage to get out of the way so that they could see him. The following evening, Joe and his brother Tom gave a dinner for the players and writers at the DiMaggio Restaurant on Fisherman's Wharf in San Francisco. Joe didn't perform any heroics in his long-awaited, much heralded homecoming, and he told local baseball writers, "It looks like the old geezer is about through. It's going to be tough to give up baseball, for I've had a lot of fun out of it. I loved every minute of it. But why kid myself? I can't go on forever."

Joe's left knee had been giving him trouble on the tour, and may have been a factor in his weak hitting to that point. He told the writers that he had been pacing himself, and added, "If this is to be my last year, I want it to be a good one. No use knocking yourself out to reach a peak too early." He then vowed, "When the bell rings, I'll be ready."

The Yankees were back at their training site in Arizona by March 27, and while DiMaggio wasn't tearing the cover off the ball, hits were beginning to come with more frequency. On March 29, he hit a bases-clearing three-run double to help beat the Cubs 7-5. The next day he slugged a triple against the Cubs, and on April 4 in El Paso he connected for a home run against the local minor league team. Stengel was quoted around this time as saying, "DiMaggio will have a big season," and the Yankee organization maintained the belief that he would be coming back in 1952. It became public many months later that when the Yankees were in Dallas on April 10 to play the Boston Braves, Del Webb sent Joe to a specialist there, and the long-term prognosis was not optimistic. The doctor reported, "DiMaggio has spurs in both shoulders, and I believe he has other arthritic involvements that will force him to quit after this season."

As training camp was winding down, Joe was getting in a groove, hitting safely in ten straight games. The team had traveled back east to engage in a three-game series with Brooklyn in New York just prior to the start of the season. It was in the first game that his hit streak was ended by Don Newcombe and Clyde King.

The Yankees would open their season on April 17 at the Stadium versus Boston, and in the elaborate pregame ceremonies, DiMaggio received his eighth World Championship ring. He then took his familiar place in center field to officially begin his 13th major league season, with young Mantle stationed beside him in right, beginning his first.

Joe kicked off his '51 campaign with an RBI single in four trips to the plate to help beat the Red Sox and Ted Williams 5-0. In the third game of the season, on April 20, he went hitless, but accumulated his first outfield assist by throwing out a runner at home plate. Over his first nine games he went only 8-for-33, and the only two hits that weren't singles were doubles.

Then near the end of April he delivered the type of performance fans were more accustomed to seeing from him. On the 27th he hammered his first home run of the year, the 350th of his career, going 2-for-3 with two RBI against the rival Red Sox.

The next day, back at the stadium, he insisted on playing despite a strained tendon in his shoulder and proceeded to have his best day of the young season. He came up in the bottom of the first with Washington already up 2-0 and hit a home run to tie the game. In the seventh he stroked a single that ended up as the game-winner, as he would go 3-for-5 with three RBIs.

Joe was being plagued with a stiff neck in late April, and an x-ray on May 1 revealed a muscle spasm that would keep him out of the lineup until May 14. He chipped in on the day of his return with two hits, two runs scored, and an RBI in the Yanks' 11-4 win over Cleveland. Six days later he hit his first home run in three weeks, his third of the year, that helped beat St. Louis 7-3. Three days after that in Detroit, Joe hit a home run that he subsequently lost when the game was called due to rain in the top of the fourth inning.

He got the home run back the next day in New York's 11-1 drubbing of the Tigers. He slumped badly over the next five games, however, going a combined 1-for-17.

DiMaggio had a rather long and busy day in a Memorial Day doubleheader against the Red Sox at Boston. In the opener he played all 15 innings, getting a triple and a single in six at-bats in the 11-10 loss. In the second contest, had added two hits including a home run and three RBI.

On June 2, the Yankees observed the tenth anniversary of the death of Lou Gehrig. Though DiMaggio, the last remaining Yankee player to have been a teammate didn't get a hit, he scored two runs to help beat Detroit 8-7. Joe played a big part in a victory on the 7th in St. Louis, in which they came from behind in the ninth. He had gone two for three with a solo home run, and was part of a ninth-inning rally in which he was intentionally walked and later scored in the 7-5 win.

Over the next week he was troubled with a sore leg and spent very little time in the lineup. On June 15 he met his ex-wife, actress Dorothy Arnold, and Joe Jr. at the airport in New York. He kissed her as she stepped from the plane but refused to discuss the possibility of a reconciliation with the assembled press. Arnold told them that she had only brought her son to New York for Father's Day. A few days later he received word from his family in San Francisco that his mother was gravely ill. He immediately flew home on June 18. Two hours after his arrival, with eight of her nine children at her bedside, Rosalie DiMaggio succumbed to cancer. Dom had missed a plane connection and arrived a half hour too late. She was laid to rest at Holy Cross Cemetery just outside San Francisco on June 21.

Two days later, Joe made his first appearance in a game since returning from the West Coast, and made his presence felt. With the Yanks down 6-4 in the ninth to the Indians at the Stadium, DiMaggio was sent up to pinch hit for Gene Woodling. He doubled to drive in the first run of the rally, scored a moment later to tie the game, and New York would go on to thrill the home crowd with a 7-6 win.

After a day on the bench followed by a pinch-hitting appearance, DiMaggio settled back into the lineup and went on a modest eight-game hitting streak. Dan Daniel wrote around this time that he thought Joe may be starting to change his mind about retiring after the season. He wrote that when the Yanks' traveling secretary was discussing the team's 1952 Spring Training itinerary, Joe seemed very interested. A week later, however, Daniel speculated that if he did return, it would likely not be as a regular. Daniel referred to " . . . the years of service on the Yankees exacting a strong physical influence, his average falling, his legs hurting, his spirit rampant but the flesh fatigued."

An incident occurred on July 7 in Boston that may have strained relations between DiMaggio and Stengel, two men whose relationship seemed rather tenuous to begin with.

On that Saturday, the Red Sox had exploded for six runs in the bottom of the first inning and Stengel decided then to pull DiMaggio and Rizzuto out of the game to rest them. Joe didn't get the message and ran out to his center field position to start the bottom of the second inning. Outfielder Johnny Hopp came out to replace him and informed him of the change, and the legend had to suffer the indignity of running back to the dugout.

When DiMaggio was asked by reporters about the incident after the game, he snapped, "I was taken out, and if you want to know more about it, see Casey Stengel." The *New York Post* reported around that time that the two men weren't speaking to each other.

Whenever Stengel gave Joe a rest it appeared to some that they were feuding and he was being benched as a result. Daniel dismissed the talk of a feud between the two and believed that Joe was more angry and frustrated at the physical woes that wouldn't allow him to perform as he had for so long. Some close to the scene said that the two just didn't hit it off, though they did appear to respect each other. A few months later, Stengel's wife commented on the reported hard feelings between Joe and her husband, saying, "They have different temperaments, but they get along fine, and all this talk just makes them hit it off better." After the July 7 game, Stengel responded to reporters' queries: "If I weren't talking to him, would I have picked him for the All-Star team despite the fact the popular poll had not placed him in a leading spot? Joe at 36 isn't as great a player as he used to be. Still, he's better than a lot of guys I have now."

In the final game of the Boston series on July 8, DiMaggio again came out very early in the game. His left calf was bothering him, and after reaching base in the second inning, he was pinch run for by Mantle. The Yankees' loss to Boston this day made five defeats in the last six games, and some felt that Joe should no longer bat fourth, nor should he play both games of doubleheaders. The season had now seemed to hit a low point for him, and he would be sitting out his final chance to perform in the Mid-Summer Classic.

After the All-Star break, DiMaggio sat out the next dozen games. He returned to the lineup on July 24, by which time his supposed heir apparent Mantle had already been sent back to the minors. His first three games back were against Cleveland, and he managed only one hit, a single, in 11 at-bats. An unnamed friend of his who was at the Stadium for the series was quoted afterward: "I am afraid the big guy is thoroughly washed up. I watched him in all three games with the Indians, and he took just three DiMaggio-style cuts at the ball." After the series, Joe said in the presence of Dan Daniel: "I will beat this thing. Mark my words, I will beat it."

In a series against the White Sox that began in New York the next day, he did start to show signs of the old Joe. He slugged a home run that helped the Yanks win 3-1 in a game that ended in the eighth due to rain. Two days later in the first game of a double-header against Chicago he had one of his bigger games of the year. He hit a home run in the first that tied the contest at two, then delivered a three-run homer in the seventh for a total of five RBI in the 8-3 win. His second RBI of the game was the 1500th of his career.

A very unusual incident occurred involving DiMaggio in the first game of the Tiger series on July 30 at home. Joe made what many called the first mental error they could recall seeing him make. In the eighth inning with one out and George Kell on second base, Steve Souchock hit a fly to center field that DiMaggio caught. He stood there a moment, then began to jog in as Kell trotted all the way around to score. Observers were shocked by the mental lapse, and the prideful superstar was unquestionably embarrassed.

He managed to atone for the transgression by producing a game-winning single in the bottom of the ninth. Yet another un-usual incident involving DiMaggio around this time was observed during pre-game warmups when he was feeding baseballs to the batting practice pitcher, prompting one writer to say, "That's the first step when a fellow quits playing and turns to coaching."

In the second game of a doubleheader on August 1, Joe had his first three-hit game since late April, driving in two runs in the 10-6 win over Detroit. A little over a week later on August 9 against Washington, his homer in the sixth tied the game up, and his triple in the seventh added the final insurance run in the 6-4 victory. After the game, Joe blew up at writers who had been critical of him dur-ing recent slumps, or had questioned him remaining in the cleanup spot.

He had long been resentful of reporters, but particularly so now that they were obligated to report his failures more frequently. The relationship that DiMaggio had with the press very likely was not like that of any athlete before or since. Some days he would talk to reporters, while other days he appeared moody and remained silent. Some writers had grown a bit tired of guessing which way he would be on a given day. Daniel had written in the spring that there wasn't one New York baseball writer who didn't like Joe. John Drebinger of the *New York Times* was a bit more harsh explaining in late July DiMaggio's penchant for giving short, surly answers to the press:

> " . . . this has been (his) attitude for a long time. In fact he rarely talks to his teammates or manager, let alone anyone remotely associated with the press. On a recent train ride following a game in Philadelphia, DiMaggio, in the Yanks' special diner, sat by himself at a table for four. It's a queer set-up, but almost everyone traveling with the Bombers is leaving the Clipper severely alone."

Bill Corum of the *New York Journal-American* wrote that DiMaggio was a "moody and temperamental fellow," yet most writers simply opted to ignore this remoteness rather than boldly attempt to invade the Greta Garbo-like shell into which he seemed to climb during slumps. Even many of the veteran New York scribes had difficulty being objective, having observed his years of inimitable grace and the level of hero-worship he had inspired.

Though there had been many dark days of late, August 13 brought a better day. While in Philadelphia for a game with the Athletics, Joe was honored at Shibe Park by the Diamond Social Club of Vineland, New Jersey. He was presented with a glass trophy, golf clubs, a plaque, and a lifetime membership to the club. He then went out and had a 3-for-5 day with a double and three runs scored. This began a five-game span in which he hit .333 with three doubles and six runs scored. It was observed at this time that despite DiMaggio's failure to hit even .270 for the season thus far, Stengel really had no better option as a cleanup hitter.

Joe suffered another indignity to which he was unaccustomed on August 25. At Cleveland, pitcher Steve Gromek walked Gene Woodling in the ninth inning to get to DiMaggio, which was the first time such a strategy had been employed against him. This surprised the 66,000 in attendance, and served as a further reminder that his stature as a hitter had declined. Joe got his revenge, though, as he singled sharply to center to drive in a run as Indians fans cheered him on. The 7-3 win also put the Yanks only a game out of first place.

Indians G.M. Hank Greenberg said to J.G. Taylor Spink shortly after:

> "You know fans in general still expect DiMaggio to play up to his old standard. If he is only average, they say, 'That guy is washed up.' You see, they will not accept the average performance from Joe. I know how they feel, and I know how Joe feels."

Greenberg also added that he felt that even at 37, Joe was still as good a center fielder as there was in the A.L. at that time.

DiMaggio started off September on a positive note, contributing with his bat in Eddie Lopat's three-hit, 4-0 victory. Along with a double, RBI, and run scored, Joe had what would be the last three-hit game of his illustrious career.

The Yankees and Joe had a tough day on September 11, dropping both ends of a doubleheader to the lowly Browns in New York and slipping a full game behind first-place Cleveland. DiMaggio went only 1-for-7 on the day and made an error in each game. In the second contest, Joe faced the ageless Satchel Paige for the final time in his career. When Paige had been signed by Veeck in July, he recalled the first time he had ever faced DiMaggio, saying that he struck him out on three pitches.

Joe played a big part in a crucial game on September 16 against the first-place Indians with Allie Reynolds opposing his ex-teammate Bob Feller. The largest crowd of the season at 68,760 had jammed the Stadium to see a battle of the league's top two teams.

In a move that had been speculated upon, DiMaggio had been dropped from his customary cleanup spot down to number five in the batting order. In the fifth inning, as they had three weeks earlier, the Indians walked a batter, this time Berra, to pitch to Joe.

With two out and two on base he made them pay once again by tripling to left center, driving Feller from the game as the fans went wild. He added a double, and the 5-1 win helped New York regain the lead by percentage points.

Joe was making news off the field as well in mid-September as he, his brother Dom, and several major leaguers agreed to play on a four-week exhibition tour of Japan headed by San Francisco Seals manager Lefty O'Doul beginning in mid-October. Joe was also spotted escorting Marlene Dietrich to the Sugar Ray Robinson-Randy Turpin boxing match at the Polo Groumds. It also seemed at this time that there was constant speculation about his plans for the 1952 season. Daniel remained confidant of his return and wrote in his *Sporting News* column of September 19, "That 'Guiseppe' will be back next season appears to be certain, even though he says he has not given retirement or staying any thought." He amended this slightly a week later, writing that if the Yankees win he may stay, but if they lose, he may feel partially at fault and quit. The general impression around the team was that he would return, though likely in a limited role.

With the season winding down, September 28 turned out to be significant for both DiMaggio and the Yankees. In the first game of the doubleheader against Boston, Reynolds tossed his second no-hitter, followed by the pennant-clinching complete game 11-3 win by Vic Raschi in Game Two. The clincher featured a three-run home run by Joe, which was the 361st and ultimately the final of his storied career. It also meant that he would be appearing in his tenth Fall Classic, tying him with Babe Ruth for the record in that category.

It was Joe's brother who made the final out that captured the Yanks' third straight pennant. The fly ball was caught by left fielder Gene Woodling, who handed the ball to Joe as they were running off the field. Woodling figured that if it was DiMaggio's last season, he should have the ball as a souvenir. Woodling had commented to Daniel about a week before regarding playing beside Joe:

> "He gives me hell if I do the wrong thing. He knows every-
> thing. He has helped me plenty for three years. Playing alongside

Joe is an education and a privilege. DiMaggio is still as good as any other centerfielder in the American League."

Upon entering the clubhouse after the pennant-clinching game, Stengel walked over to DiMaggio and said, "Joe, I want to thank you for everything you did." Later, the manager told the writers that the Yankees couldn't have won it without him. He spoke of how important Joe's fielding and baserunning were in many victories, and added, "I would say, next to his brother Dom, he's still the best fielder in the league."

Two days later, on September 30, the Yankees' final regular-season game took place and resulted in a 3-0 shutout over Boston. In his first at-bat, DiMaggio stroked a single off Harley Hisner, pitching in what would be his only major league game. Joe was then replaced in center field by Archie Wilson. Thus concluded his 1951 regular season, and many others besides Stengel felt he had a far greater impact on the team than his .263 batting average, 12 home runs, and 72 RBI might indicate. DiMaggio also held a very prominent place in many lifetime statistical categories as the active leader in hits, doubles, triples, home runs, runs scored, and RBI. The Yankees had a three-day layoff awaiting the winner of the N.L. playoff. Once concluded, the '51 Fall Classic was finally able to get underway at Yankee Stadium on October 4 versus the neighboring Giants.

DiMaggio's bat was very quiet in the first three games as he went a combined 0-for11. He did make a very noteworthy play in the outfield in the second inning of Game Two, as he raced over to cut off a Monte Irvin liner deep in left center field and made a great throw to the infield to hold him to a single.

DiMaggio's old friend, Lefty O'Doul, whom he would be touring Japan with in a couple of weeks was in attendance at the first few Series games. O'Doul was quoted as saying of Joe: "He looked terrible, really. He was doing all the things he used to tell his brother Vince not to do, lunging, finishing up off balance, swinging too hard."

O'Doul spoke to him on the phone and gave him a bit of advice to help break him out his postseason slump. Ty Cobb also called DiMaggio at Toots Shor's and advised him to move his right foot closer to the plate.

The advice from the old hitting masters seemed to pay dividends in Game Four. He broke what was then an 0 for twelve streak by singling off Sal Maglie in the third inning.

Then in his next at-bat in the fifth inning, he tagged Maglie for a towering two-run home run into the upper deck in left field. The home run was his eighth in World Series competition. The Yanks prevailed 6-2 in the game to now tie the Series at two.

DiMaggio had switched to using a "Babe Ruth" model bat this game, which was one ounce lighter than his regular model. Maglie told reporters that the home run came on a low, inside curve. He also said graciously, "If somebody had to hit a homer off me, I'm sure glad it was Joe DiMaggio. Joe's a great guy and has taken alot of abuse. He means a lot to that ballclub."

He continued his hot hitting the next afternoon in Game Five as the Yankees as a team exploded offensively. Joe singled in the third to score Woodling; singled again in the fourth; and doubled to left in the seventh to score both Woodling and Rizzuto. He ended the day 3-for-5 with three RBIs as the Yankees shellacked the Giants 13-1. A female admirer sent Joe an orchid after the game.

In Game Six on October 10 back at Yankee Stadium, DiMaggio achieved a milestone by appearing in his 51st World Series game, breaking Frankie Frisch's record of 50, set in 1934. Having swung a hot bat and facing lefty pitcher Dave Koslo, Joe was intentionally walked twice in his first three times at bat. After the second free pass in the sixth inning, he was driven home on Bauer's bases-clearing triple.

In what would turn out to be the final time he would swing a bat in anger in the Yankee uniform, Joe DiMaggio muscled a double to right field to lead off the eighth inning. Gil McDougald then came up and laid down a bunt to attempt to move him over to third, but pitcher Larry Jansen managed to make a nice fielding play to nail Joe at third. As he jogged back to the dugout he was given a tremendous ovation by the crowd, as they suspected that this could well be the final game Joe would play. The applause was repeated as he took his place in center field for the ninth inning. The Yankees hung on to win 4-3 to clinch as DiMaggio had now been part of a remarkable nine World Championship teams in his 13 seasons. Ed McAuley of the *Cleveland News* would write, "I hope he calls it a career while the cheers are still fresh in his memory."

A few days after the conclusion of the 1951 Series, Joe stopped by the Yankee offices at 745 5th Ave. to discuss his plans with owner Dan Topping. He reportedly told Topping that he felt as though he played long enough, but the chief executive asked him to think about it for the next few months. Before departing for the Japanese tour, DiMaggio spent one day in California visiting his son, and it was around this time that he was said to have received an offer to manage Portland of the Pacific Coast League. He insisted he had no desire to manage in either the minors or the majors. Joe Reichler of the Associated Press reported that as Joe was getting on the plane for California, he said he had played his last game of big-league baseball.

DiMaggio and the touring squad boarded a plane on October 15 and would be stopping over in Hawaii for a couple of exhibitions against a team made up mostly of military players. Joe was heading a team that included brother Dom; Yankee teammates Lopat and Martin; Ferris Fain, Bobby Shantz, and Mel Parnell among the more noteworthy. They arrived in Tokyo a few days later to a tremendous welcome. An estimated crowd of close to one million people lined the streets as the American players were paraded by in open cars. Many waved American and Japanese flags, and some even threw flowers at Joe's car.

In the first game on October 20, the U.S. team beat the Yomiuri Giants 7-0 in front of a standing room only crowd of 50,000. Joe was cheered wildly in each of his three trips to the plate, in which he got one hit and walked. The next day against the Mianichi Orions, both Joe and Dom hit home runs. Joe was rooming with Billy Martin during the tour, and Yankee broadcaster Mel Allen had urged him to try to persuade DiMaggio to play in 1952.

As expected, the Americans were having little difficulty beating the Japanese teams. In the midst of sweeping a three-game series in Osaka, a Japanese reporter asked DiMaggio on November 3 if he planned to retire. He replied that Topping had asked him not to discuss the matter until he returned to the U.S. In his last game on the tour on November 10, he hit a 400-foot home run at Meiji Park in Tokyo to help beat Japan's Central League All-Stars 3-2. He then departed for the States a few days ahead of the rest of the team, saying that business matters that required his attention forced him to leave early. Back in Hollywood a few days later visiting his son again, he became agitated over reporters constantly questioning him on his plans for 1952. "It's my decision to make and I'll make it when I'm ready," he barked.

DiMaggio received high praise from a couple of young Yankee teammates around this time. Gene Woodling, touring with Gil Hodges' barnstorming team through the South expressed sincere hope that Joe would come back to play in 1952. " . . . He's got a lot of baseball left, in my opinion. He can play the outfield with any of them in the game today."

Gil McDougald, who had been fortunate in his first big-league season to have the opportunity to observe the great man up close added: "DiMaggio is one great guy, and he was swell about helping a new fellow along. But what a student of the game! He asks more questions than the rookies."

In late November, Boston writer Bob Ajemian reported that a DiMaggio -Ted Williams trade was actually being discussed. He wrote that Joe had supposedly been asked, and indicated that playing in a smaller park like Fenway might be a good way to extend his career. He was also said to be willing to play left field beside brother Dom.

Bill Veeck said in early December that Joe, not coming forth with a decision on his plans was holding up several potential trades. He said that if Joe did retire, the Yanks might still try to acquire Ted, using younger players as bait. If Joe stayed, these players might be used in other deals.

On December 4, DiMaggio arrived in Phoenix to discuss the matter with Del Webb, and they later traveled to New York together to meet with Topping. Joe checked into the Hotel Madison, and Webb and Topping spent the entire evening of December 10 trying to convince him to remain active as a player for one more season. A press conference was scheduled for the following afternoon at the Yankee executive offices on 5th Ave., at which Joe would finally make his intentions known to the world.

On the afternoon of December 11, the room in which the press conference was to be held was mobbed with reporters and photographers. The proceedings began with a formal statement read by Yankees press secretary Arthur Patterson informing those assembled of DiMaggio's decision to retire. Joe himself then took center stage, and included in his statement was:

> "Old injuries caught up with me, and brought on new ones. I found that it was a chore for me to straighten up after I had retrieved a ground ball. In short, I was not pleased with myself any longer, and all the fun had gone out of playing the game. When baseball is no longer fun, it's no longer a game. And so I've played my last game of ball."

With that, the 13-season major league career of Joseph Paul DiMaggio and his accomplishments on the field of play were cast in stone for all time.

Topping announced the next day that DiMaggio's uniform No. 5 would be retired, joining Ruth's No. 3, and Gehrig's No. 4. He also said Joe's uniform, glove, and bat that he homered with in Game Four of the '51 Series would be presented to the Hall of Fame. Daniel had written that just as Babe Ruth's retirement marked the end of an era, so would Joe's.

Topping revealed also that DiMaggio was being hired for 1952 as a television commentator for the team, conducting pregame and postgame interviews. His contract called for him to be paid $50,000 for the job.

Upon the announcement of his brother's retirement from the game, Dom stated:

> "I'm glad to see Joe quit for his own sake. It was too tough for him physically. He never complained, but he was handicapped.

JOE DIMAGGIO AND MICKEY MANTLE. *The legendary careers of Joe DiMaggio and Mickey Mantle were traveling in opposite directions during the 1951 season.*

His muscles wouldn't respond. Joe made the right decision. Joe didn't play too much in Japan, and when he did, it was an effort for him . . . injuries caught up with (him). I think it was his back and shoulder and neck maybe that bothered him most."

Dom also made the observation that during the past season, Joe was letting go of the bat with his right hand on the follow through of his swing. "It was very obvious to me. He just couldn't hold the bat correctly."

Writer Corum of the *New York Journal-American* was very harsh in his assessment of DiMaggio's final season:

"He didn't have it any more and he knew it, and knowing it, he didn't want to be out where all could see that he didn't have it. I used to turn my eyes away from the TV screen at times late last season when he came to bat."

Ty Cobb however, as opinionated as ever, presented another view of DiMaggio.

Contacted by writer Jack McDonald on the occasion of his sixty-fifth birthday, the all-time batting champ commented on Joe's retirement:

> "I think DiMaggio quit a year, maybe two too soon . . . I saw Joe in the World Series (on) TV only two and one-half months ago and he was still the standout center fielder in baseball. And his hitting in the last three games proved he still had it."

Three days after his historic announcement, Joe DiMaggio flew back to his native California to begin his new life as an ex-ballplayer. At a baseball banquet in Boston three days after that, Phil Rizzuto revealed for the first time publicly that Joe was fairly definite about his retirement plans many months prior. Rizzuto told the crowd that sometime in the middle of the season, Yogi Berra was kidding Joe about retiring, saying, "You'll never quit." DiMaggio looked up at Berra and said, "If I play one game with the Yankees next season, I'll give you $500. You don't have to give me anything." Rizzuto was the only other person present at the time as the two men shook hands on it.

On the day that Joe had made it official, Stengel then proclaimed young Mantle to be his starting center fielder for the upcoming season. Contacted at his Commerce, Oklahoma home and informed of what had transpired, he said, "It will be impossible for anyone to take his place—he's that great. But they can count on me doing the best I can."

On Opening Day at Yankee Stadium in April of 1952, it was DiMaggio who threw out the first pitch, as Mantle indeed was occupying his old turf in center field.

Mantle was on his way to stardom, while DiMaggio was well on his way to Cooperstown.

14

BREAKING THE TIE:

Hatfields vs. McCoys—New York Style

OF ALL THE RIVALRIES IN THE HISTORY of professional sports, few can match the intensity and passion evoked by partisans of the Brooklyn Dodgers and their crosstown enemies, the New York Giants in the 1950s. The animosity between the teams and their followers, not terribly unlike a holy war, reached its zenith in late summer and early fall of 1951 with one of the most incredible, implausible climaxes in the game's history.

Many months before that conclusive moment that holds its place as one of the rare moments of all time in baseball history, the overwhelming majority of experts picked the Dodgers and Giants to finish one-two in the N.L. standings. No one could have predicted, however, that it would take three additional games in order to separate the two.

Adding to the rivalry were the histories of the two men who would be leading their respective teams from the dugout. Leo Durocher of the Giants had piloted the Dodgers from 1939 up until his one-year suspension after the 1946 season by Commissioner Chandler for conduct detrimental to baseball. He returned for 1948, but was replaced at mid-season by Burt Shotton. One year later he took over the rival Giants. Charlie Dressen, who had been a coach for Brooklyn for many years under Durocher had just been appointed to take over for Shotton in late November of 1950. Dressen, it was believed, was anxious to prove to the baseball world that he had every bit as shrewd a managerial mind as his former boss Durocher.

LEO DUROCHER. *Leo Durocher is rewarded by son Chris for a job well done in October of 1951. Courtesy of National Baseball Library*

Both teams had come up a tad shy of the N.L. pennant in 1950, but certainly close enough to have plenty of reason to be optimistic for '51. Brooklyn had agonizingly lost out to the surprising Phillies on the final day of the season, and the Giants had finished just three games behind the Dodgers. New York had overcome a very mediocre first half to win 50 of their final 72 games. Few of the baseball writers gave the Phillies any significant chance to repeat, and of the 204 polled in early April, 49% picked the Giants to win, while 34% favored Brooklyn. The Dodgers lineup appeared a bit more stable with all starting positions virtually set, with names such as Campanella, Hodges, Robinson, Reese, Snider, and Furillo. Some also speculated that with the power they possessed and the cozy confines of Ebbets Field, they could threaten the N.L. team record for home runs with 221 set by the 1947 Giants. The Giants, on the other hand were considering switching Monte Irvin to first base full time, with Whitey Lockman as the left fielder, and there was concern that second baseman Eddie Stanky was getting old at 34. They were hopeful that Hank Thompson could repeat his performance of 1950 at third base, but in fact there was destined to be considerable lineup shuffling at the Polo Grounds. The consensus in the Giants camp as the season approached was that they could win if they could hit.

Buzzie Bavasi, who had taken over the general manager duties for the Dodgers in the wake of Branch Rickey's departure proclaimed before the season "We feel that we are the club to beat, and the Giants are the boys who will prove the most troublesome."

Recently deposed Brooklyn manager Shotton said from his Florida home that the Giants were the only team with a chance to beat the Dodgers. Reds general manager Warren Giles conceded that his team had little chance to top Brooklyn, whom he felt was the clear favorite. Even Eddie Sawyer, manager of the defending N.L. champion Phillies felt that the loss of pitcher Curt Simmons severely hurt their chances, and predicted a Brooklyn pennant. Dressen was unquestionably under pressure as big things were expected.

The Giants opened their 1951 season on April 17 in Boston with a fine performance from Larry Jansen in a 4-0 win. The Dodgers on that day started off on a down note with a 5-2 loss to Robin Roberts and the Phillies. Three days later, New York, who had won two of its first three was set to begin a three-game series at the Polo Grounds against the 1-1 Dodgers. It was this day, April 20, that it all started to fall apart for Durocher's squad.

In the first game, Don Newcombe scored a decisive 7-3 victory; Ralph Branca followed up the next afternoon with a 7-3 win of his own; and Newcombe came back and was credited with a win with three innings of relief work to complete the sweep on the Giants' own turf. The loss in the final game was particularly tough to take, as Carl Furillo hit a home run in the tenth off Sal Maglie that won the game 4-3. Durocher, who had managed Furillo in Brooklyn insisted that he couldn't hit a sidearm pitch from a right hander, which is what Maglie threw. Maglie had struck him out earlier in the game.

New York then took the train down to Philadelphia for a brief three-game trip and returned home the night of April 25 having been swept by the defending N.L. champs.

Without missing a beat, the Giants dropped both games of a two-game set the next two days with the Braves to extend their losing streak to nine. Everyone connected with the team, from the front office, to the players, to the fans, and even the beat writers, were shocked at the revolting turn of events. They seemed to be slumping in virtually every phase of the game.

Before the situation could improve, the Giants had three games scheduled at Ebbets Field on the last three days of April, which dug their hole a bit deeper. With the help of a Jackie Robinson home run in the seventh inning of the first game, the Dodgers handed New York their tenth straight loss. The next day, the figure reached 11 as the vaunted Brooklyn power, with two home runs by Snider and one from Hodges, contributed to a 6-3 win. On one of Snider's homers, Jansen had knocked him down with a high, hard one just before Duke put it in the parking lot. The Dodgers had now moved into a tie for first with Boston and St. Louis, while the Giants were alone in the basement with a pitiful 2-12 record.

Over the winter, Leo had uttered his famous quote: "Nice guys finish last," yet this spring he was observed to be a nicer, more mellow person than he had seemed in the past. Some credited the influence of his wife, movie actress Laraine Day. *The Sporting News* editorialized in its May 9 issue that they hoped Leo wouldn't see his team's last place standing as proof of his philosophy.

Finally on April 30, amidst considerable bench-jockeying and trash-talking from both teams, the Giants were able to put an end to the dreaded streak. They came out strong, scoring all eight of their runs in the first two innings, then had to quell several potential rallies the rest of the way as Maglie finally got his first win. Despite the victory, Arthur Daley was completely writing off the Giants in his *New York Times* column the next day: "It would take a miracle for them to win the championship now," and "The team that is sitting prettiest right now is Brooklyn, which had everything except pitching and now seems to have that also."

The Giants were on the verge of reversing their fortunes, but changes would occur.

On May 1, catcher Westrum broke his finger and was replaced by backup Ray Noble. A thirty-two-year-old former Negro Leaguer described as being built like an Army tank, Noble was in his first year in the major leagues. Durocher also dropped a slumping Monte Irvin from the cleanup spot to eighth, and replaced him in the order with Hank Thompson. Maglie was pitching like the all-star he would be, throwing a one-hitter against Pittsburgh on May 4, and holding St. Louis to five hits in a 17-2 win in his next start. Maglie had a well-earned reputation for the brush back pitch, and in an article that featured him in the May 5 issue of the *Saturday Evening Post*, he was quoted:

> "Sure, I'll throw at anybody. That's part of the game. I've got to do it to protect myself against hitters leaning on my curve. I don't want to hurt anybody, but guys who try to take a toehold on me are going to get knocked down."

The sparkling defensive work of shortstop Alvin Dark and shortstop Eddie Stanky was also an important factor in the Giants making their slow, steady climb back to .500, winning 11 of 14 after the losing streak ended. Three of the losses were near misses, all coming in the tenth inning.

By May 21, Durocher moved Monte Irvin back to the outfield, saying he just did not have the hands for first base, and installed Whitey Lockman there. The big change however, came when Leo, seeking to further spark the team and upgrade the outfield defense promoted just-turned 20-year-old Willie Mays, who was tearing up the American Association with Minneapolis. Bobby Thomson was moved from center field to left upon the arrival of Mays. The move seemed to have an immediate impact on Thomson at the plate. He was hitting .229 at the time but got five hits in his next 11 at-bats, several of them in key situations. The Giants now went with a fairly set lineup, rather than platooning, and also had Westrum back behind the plate.

In Mays' second game with the Giants, in Philadelphia on May 26, they finally reached the elusive .500 plateau behind Jansen's seven-hit shutout. In all, they had compiled an 18-9 record for the month of May, but were still only in fifth place. The Dodgers, who had taken over first place seemingly for good on May 13 closed out the month with a winning percentage of .615 to that point.

By early June, Brooklyn seemed to have all of the elements: hitting, baserunning, defense, and pitching. They had the league leaders in batting (Robinson), home runs (Hodges), and RBI (Snider), and Preacher Roe already had seven wins without a defeat.

Hodges' 20th home run came on June 14, not having hit his 20th in 1950 until late August. Actually ahead of Ruth's 1927 pace at various times, some were speculating that he might have a shot at the hallowed 60 mark. As for his slugging partner, left-handed hitting Snider, he was thought by some to be the 'next Musial.'

With their 6-3 win over the Reds in Cincinnati on June 12, the Giants moved into second place, but three days later the Dodgers made a move that almost seemed to make it all academic. It was June 15 that Brooklyn pulled off an eight-player trade with the Cubs in which they acquired outstanding outfielder Andy Pafko. Along with Pafko, Brooklyn received Johnny Schmitz, Rube Walker, and

Wayne Terwilliger, sending Chicago Gener Hermanski, Bruce Edwards, Joe Hatten, and Eddie Miskis. But it was Pafko, who had hit 36 home runs for the Cubs the previous season, who was the key to the deal for the Dodgers. Inserting him in left field, Brooklyn could now boast of one of the better outfields of all time in terms of all-around ability.

The trade was called "the big steal of 1951," and "earth-jarring." It was considered a brilliant coup by young general manager Bavasi, and was thought to have sewed up the pennant for the Dodgers.

It served to correct the only weak spot on an otherwise great team, and they did so without sacrificing any of the full-time regulars. In addition, Pafko was considered a gate attraction, and Walter O'Malley thought he might help to lure as many as an extra 250,000 fans through the Ebbets Field turnstiles by season's end.

Upon learning of the deal, Pafko now believed he had a great chance of getting to the World Series after spending several seasons deep in the second division with the Cubs.

He added, "I'll tell you what is probably the greatest thing of all about this deal as far as I'm concerned. Now I don't have to bat against Newcombe any more. I'd have to call him the toughest pitcher I've ever had to face."

The trade occurred while the two clubs were playing each other in Chicago, and when newly traded Gene Hermanski saw his ex-teammates the next day, he told them, "This means you guys will lose the pennant. Without me in left field, you haven't got a chance." In his first game against his old team that day, Pafko hit a home run, but unfortunately for Brooklyn, Edwards, part of the deal also, hit a home run and drove in four runs to help the Cubs win 6-4.

Durocher squawked at this time that he had offered the Cubs four players, including three regulars for Pafko at the Winter Meetings the previous December. Bobby Thomson was later revealed to be one of the regulars. Leo claimed he would have made the trade even if just to prevent the Dodgers from getting Pafko, but he was quickly turned down by Frankie Frisch. On paper, the Giants were now outclassed by Brooklyn at almost every position.

Preacher Roe, the Dodgers' lean, left-handed hillbilly from Arkansas swelled his record to 10-0 on June 21 in what was shaping up to be his career season. The eccentric hurler who refused to fly in a plane was giving Newcombe competition as the ace of the Brooklyn staff.

As good a month as the Giants had in June, going 17-11, they made no dent in the Dodgers' lead, with Brooklyn posting an 18-10 record in the same span. The Giants' resurgence in the previous two months had been fueled by several factors: their ability to produce an everyday player like young Mays from their minor league system; inserting Don Mueller in the outfield when Bobby Thomson slumped; utilizing backup Bill Rigney or Davey Williams at second base when Stanky needed a rest; and getting decent performances from Dave Koslo and Sheldon Jones when they inserted them in the rotation. Still, their deficit of five-and-a-half games at the beginning of July was one game worse than it had been at the beginning of June.

The two teams were set to engage in a three-game series beginning with a doubleheader on the Independence Day holiday. Thirty thousand fans were said to be turned away from Ebbets Field on this Wednesday afternoon, but the sellout crowd that did attend likely felt they had gotten their money's worth. Sal Maglie pitched shutout ball for seven innings, taking a 4-0 lead into the bottom of the eighth. The Dodgers then rallied with three in the eighth and one in the ninth to tie. Thomson, on a recent hot streak, hit his fourth home run in four games in the eleventh to give New York a 5-4 lead. Then in the bottom of the inning, Snider doubled, Robinson singled, and catcher Noble threw wild on a pickoff attempt. Roe, who was on in relief, laid down a squeeze bunt to score Robinson for the 6-5 win. Brooklyn came back in the second game behind the strong pitching of Ralph Branca to win 4-2 to complete the sweep of the Fourth of July twin bill.

The Giants failed to avoid a series sweep the following day as Newcombe hurled a complete game 8-4 win. Hodges' 27th home run now put him five games ahead of Ruth's 1927 pace.

GIL HODGES. *Gil Hodges slides home safely. In 1951 it was written that Hodges "was sturdily built and durable as the village blacksmith." It was also observed that his enormous hand barely it into a standard first baseman's mitt.*

Durocher and Carl Furillo were carrying on a bitter feud at this time. Furillo had even turned down Durocher's wife's request to appear on her television show. The right fielder was claiming that Leo was having his pitchers throw at him, and recalled one day in 1950 when Durocher said they would, and Carl did end up getting hit in the head in that game. Furillo had said in late May that the next time a Giant pitcher throws at his head he would walk into the dugout and take a punch at Leo. He reiterated this at the beginning of the July series, saying, "If it happens again, I'll get him. For every day I spend in the hospital, he'll spend two."

In the wake of the Dodger sweep, New York writer Joe King wrote that while virtually all of baseball conceded the pennant to Brooklyn, many older Dodger fans are doing no such thing. Because of the team's history, they were suspicious of big leads at mid-season and knew that they could be blown. In 1946, Brooklyn had a lead of seven and one-half games in early July but were caught by St. Louis. In '42 they had a ten-and-one-half game lead on August 5 but also lost to the Cardinals.

Dressen and Durocher engaged in a bit of verbal sniping in the press in mid-July.

Dressen compared the current Dodger team to the 1941 team, of which he had been a coach and Leo managed. He said, "All I know is that when we won the pennant in 1941, everyone said that it was the greatest club Brooklyn ever had. But this is a better club than the 1941 team." Durocher responded, "This is all I know, the '41 team won the pennant. That's something that the '51 Dodgers haven't done yet. Another thing. This Dressen— he talks. He's gonna do this, he's gonna do that, he's gonna do a lot of things. He's on top so he can afford to talk. I can't talk. I'm not on top."

Toward the end of July, New York began winning again, capturing seven of the final nine games of the month. During that span, Durocher had recorded his 1,000th managerial victory on July 25 at just 45 years old. One significant lineup change during this time saw Hank Thompson sent down to Ottawa, with Bobby Thomson replacing him at third base beginning on July 20. Thomson had come up to the majors as a third baseman from Jersey City in 1946, but hadn't played the position since. He had been hitting only .237 up to that point of the season, but hit .354 over the next 16 days.

Pirates broadcaster Pie Traynor, their great third baseman of the 1920s and '30s called the Giants infield combination of Lockman, Davey Williams, Dark, and Thomson the fastest infield he had ever seen.

The foot speed that Bobby Thomson possessed is one aspect of his game that tends to be forgotten. Durocher believed that he was the fastest runner in the National League, and in 1950 had proposed that he and Braves rookie Sam Jethroe have a race, with the loser donating $1,000 to charity. The idea was discussed with the owners of the two teams, but commissioner Chandler ultimately nixed the idea, fearing that it would encourage wagering.

Early August brought no new hope to the Giants in their implausible quest to make a run at the pennant. On the morning of August 3, the standings showed Brooklyn with a season-high ten-game advantage. Their best chance to chip away at the seemingly insurmountable lead would come on August 8 as they began a three-game series in the borough of Brooklyn. The first two games were to be part of a doubleheader that Wednesday, and New York had the task of facing Dodgers ace Preacher Roe. The lefty came out after only two innings, and was relieved by Carl Erskine, who went the rest of the way and gave up only five hits and one run. Brooklyn prevailed easily by a margin of 7-2, to seemingly add another nail to the Giants' coffin. The second game of the twinbill was much more hotly contested, requiring ten innings for the decision. Maglie started for New York but was ineffective and lasted only four innings. It came down to the bottom of the tenth tied at six with lefty Dave Koslo pitching for the Giants, and Billy Cox singled in Pafko to win.

The final meeting of the two teams in this series took place on Thursday, August 9, and turned out to be a wild affair. A new league record was set in the game with a combined total of 24 walks. Irvin connected for a two-run homer in the first off Branca, who was removed in the second inning after walking four. Campanella's second home run of the game in the seventh broke a tie and ended up as the winning margin in the 6-5 game. The Giants had been dominated in almost every phase of the game and suffered an utterly devastating sweep at the hands of the Dodgers in what was mistakenly called the "last crucial series of the season." As the last out was recorded that Thursday, Brooklyn now had a 12-and-a-half game lead over New York, 15 ahead in the loss column. Joe King wrote:

"It seems such a cinch that nobody but the Dodgers can beat the Dodgers. Only through a cataclysmic blowup could they allow an inferior competitor to sneak in, and this Dodger team is so deep in great men, so zestful in spirit that it hardly can collapse."

—*The Sporting News* August 15, 1951

The Dodgers were being hailed as a work of art started years before by Larry MacPhail, carried on by Branch Rickey, and elevated to their current standing by the administration of Walter O'Malley. Dan Daniel wrote a column entitled: "Dodgers Waltzing to Easiest Flag in Brooklyn's Big League History."

The day after the series concluded in Brooklyn, both teams had their games cancelled due to rain. On Saturday, August 11, the Giants trekked down to Philadelphia and the slide continued further as they were promptly shut out 4-0 by Robin Roberts. At the same time back in Brooklyn, the Dodgers were engaging in a doubleheader with Boston.

They proceeded to blow out the Braves 8-1, and as that game concluded along with the Giants' loss, Brooklyn now stood a whopping season-high 13-and-a-half games up on second-place New York. The fact that the Dodgers' 8-4 loss in the second game of the doubleheader with Boston brought the lead back to 13 games seemed of little consolation. The pennant aspirations of Durocher's team were hardly worth discussing. The three-game series between the Giants and Dodgers at the Polo Grounds coming up on August 14-16 wouldn't realistically appear to have pennant implications, but would merely be played for personal pride against a bitter crosstown rival.

The Giants were able to halt their losing streak by sweeping a doubleheader with the Phillies on August 12, and also topped them 5-2 in the closing game of the series the next day. The Dodgers closed out their series with Boston with two wins on those dates. Now as the first- and second-place teams were set to square off for three on Tuesday, the 14th in Harlem, they were separated by a bulky 12-and-a-half game margin.

Durocher surprised many by naming reliever George Spencer as his starter in the opening game. He would be opposed by Erv

Palica, who was making his first start since being publicly ripped for "choking" by Dressen in recent performances. Dressen was harshly criticized by local and national sportswriters for his handling of the young pitcher. Palica did not help his cause this day when he gave up three runs in the first inning including home runs to Don Mueller and Whitey Lockman. Palica was not allowed to come out for the second inning. Spencer, meanwhile, took a shutout into the eighth inning and came away with a complete-game 4-2 win.

The following day shaped up as a pitcher's duel between Jim Hearn and Ralph Branca, who both went the distance. Mays made a good catch followed by a spectacular throw to nail Billy Cox at the plate in the eighth inning to keep the score knotted at one.

Then in the bottom of the frame, Wes Westrum hit a home run with Mays on base that ultimately secured the victory for Hearn and the Giants, 3-1. The final game of the series turned out to be another low-scoring, pitching-dominated affair between two tough customers, Maglie and Newcombe. With the scored tied 1-1 in the bottom of the seventh inning, Newcombe uncorked a wild pitch that allowed Thomson to score from third, and the contest ended 2-1. The Giants had avenged the sweep by the Dodgers from the week before, but still stood nine-and-one-half games off the pace.

Now on a six-game roll, New York went back down to Philadelphia and proceeded to sweep the Phils in a three-game weekend matchup. Jansen had tossed a four-hit shutout in the second game, and the final win saw Thomson hit a key two-run homer in the eighth to tie. With Boston beating Brooklyn this day, the Giants were now eight back. After a day off they were back at home to host the Reds for two at the Polo Grounds, and each game would feature heroics on their part. On August 21 they scored six runs on three homers in the eighth to win their tenth straight by a margin of 7-4. This was now their longest win streak since Durocher had taken over the team in mid-July of 1948. The following day they edged the Reds by a score of 4-3, scoring the winning run in the eighth inning for the third straight game. The Dodgers swept a doubleheader from St. Louis this day to put their lead back at eight games.

Rain over the next few days would only allow the Giants to host Stan Musial's Cardinal's for one game on August 24. It turned out to be a see-saw battle that lasted nearly three-and-a-half hours, but the Giants weaved their magic again by coming from behind and scoring two in the ninth to win 6-5. Over in Brooklyn, Ralph Branca was striking out ten Cubs in a three-hit, 1-0 shutout. Those same Cubs were next on the Polo Grounds schedule, and the Giants had the extremely tough task of attempting to extend their winning streak in back-to-back doubleheaders on August 26 and 27.

The first twin-bill, a Sunday afternoon affair saw still more heroics in the opener. Westrum again hit a key home run, this time in the ninth to win by one, 5-4. This was the eighth win of the streak that was won by a margin of one run. Jim Hearn delivered with a five-hit 5-1 win in the second game, with Mays pulling off a steal of home. The next afternoon, Larry Jansen gamely pitched all 12 innings of the first contest as the Giants squeaked out a 5-4 win to extend the streak to a remarkable 15 games. The highly unlikely back-to-back sweep was complete in Game Two as Al Corwin tossed a complete game six-hit 6-3 win. Called up at mid-season, the rookie pitcher had extended his own personal unbeaten streak to five games. Brooklyn meanwhile, had split two straight doubleheaders with Pittsburgh, and their lead had now dwindled to a mere five games.

The Giants' resurgence was being called one of the greatest team efforts in history. It had captured the interest of fans all around the country, and many were now actively pulling for the Giants. By late August, fans in both the Polo Grounds and Ebbets Field were commonly seen with radios to keep track of how their rivals were faring. Durocher would say that the Giants' 4-2 victory over the Dodgers back in August in the first game of that particular series gave his team the idea that Brooklyn could be beat.

Two days before that game, Leo had reinserted Eddie Stanky in the lineup after replacing him briefly with Davey Williams. Durocher knew that Stanky was just the type of player who could spark the team, and as it would turn out, his first day back in the lineup was the beginning of the win streak. Stanky had been described by one writer earlier in the season as having a will to win that was "almost hysterical." Durocher also credited Monte Irvin with supplying many key hits, and called him one of the most underrated players in the National League.

Finally on August 28 with Pittsburgh at New York to begin a three-game set, the longest winning streak in the N.L. since the Cubs won 21 in 1935 came to a close. The manner in which the game was lost was painful, as errors by Stanky and Mueller in the eighth inning allowed the only two runs of the contest to score.

Also, Thomson missed a home run by about a foot that Durocher swore would have changed the entire complexion of the game. In their final two games of the month, the Giants split with Pittsburgh while the Dodgers were sweeping three games with the Reds. On the morning of September 1, the standings showed Brooklyn to have a seven-game lead with a quick two-game trip to the Polo Grounds for that day and the next.

New York took advantage, sweeping the two games convincingly by scores of 8-1 and 11-2. In Saturday's kickoff, Maglie cruised, going the distance, while Branca had his troubles and was gone after four. It would seem noteworthy in weeks to come that Bobby Thomson homered off Branca in this game. The Giant win also featured a triple play off the bat of Pee Wee Reese started by Alvin Dark, and three home runs by unlikely slugger Mueller. The 11-2 Giants win on Sunday came at the expense of an ineffective Newcombe, who was also beaten by a six-hitter from Jim Hearn. Newcombe was also ejected along with Dressen and Robinson in the seventh after a heated argument with umpire Al Barlick. Thomson later homered again, and Mueller inexplicably added two more for five in two days. He had already hit one in the game, and when Monte Irvin informed him just before going to bat in the eighth inning that his wife just had a baby boy back in St. Louis, he slugged one for his new son.

New York had now shaved the lead back to five again, with 28 days left in the season. Just six days later, the teams would engage in their last regularly scheduled meeting with two games in Brooklyn. In the first game, September 8, Newcombe had his best stuff and held the Giants to just two hits in an embarrassing 9-0 game.

They dusted themselves off the next day, however, as Maglie became the first N.L. pitcher to get his 20th victory in a tight 2-1 ballgame. Branca again took the loss, surrendering the only two New York runs on an Irvin home run in the fourth. As they had so many times in recent weeks, the Giants were saved by one of their effective weapons—the home run. Also, Thomson had begun a key double play in the eighth inning to quell a Dodger rally. Durocher said later of him, "There isn't a better third baseman in the league right now."

In the wake of the split of the two games between the two, Brooklyn beat writer Joe King, in his column, went into a lengthy explanation regarding the almost certain end to the pennant race:

> "The Dodgers, who just about sewed up the flag in the split with the Giants over the September 8-9 weekend headed west in a wonderful position to tune up their pitching and rest up their ailing for the World Series. They had an easy schedule for the remainder of the term, and Dressen could afford to give his pitchers an extra day between starts, and to bench any regular who showed any wear and tear of the long campaign."

King then went into the simple mathematics that if the Giants were to win all 16 remaining games, Brooklyn would have to lose eight of their 19 to blow the pennant. Ken Smith, covering the Giants, basically conceded on their behalf in the September 19 *Sporting News*, and was already looking ahead to next season:

> "Although the Giants started too late to overtake the Dodgers, they nevertheless wrote an impressive accomplishment in the season's records with a 16-game winning streak, longest in the majors . . . all in all, the Durochermen have gained the respect of the league in their gallant but futile late-season bid, and stack up as formidable pennant threats for 1952."

Bill Roeder of the *New York World-Telegram and Sun* wrote, "The only question left for the Dodgers seems to be whether they have the ability and the confidence to win the World Series."

Over the next several days, the Brooklyn lead shuffled back and forth between five and six games as time was running out on New York. They did clinch at least second place in their 5-2 win over Chicago, but when Durocher was asked about its significance he snapped: "What good is that? You either win the pennant or you lose."

Then by September 17, by virtue of their sweep of a double-header with the Pirates the day before and Brooklyn's loss to Chicago this day, the margin dropped to four. The Dodgers lost more than just the game to the Cubs as Campanella was beaned by Turk Lown and carried off on a stretcher. In the five games Al Walker filled in for him, he was hitless and committed one error. A Giant win and Dodger loss on the 18th further reduced it to three.

In the Giant 6-5 victory over the Reds that day, Hank Edwards, whom Brooklyn had sold to the Reds in mid-July, gained a slight measure of revenge over the team that had dispatched him to the second division, by failing to hit in a clutch situation. Down one run to the Giants in the ninth, the Reds had the tying and winning run on. Edwards, pinch hitting, hit into a force to end the game. In this situation, he had a genuine opportunity to tack one more loss on to New York, which in the end could have made all the difference.

There was no significant change in status until six days later on September 24, when with Brooklyn idle, New York beat Boston 4-3 to get to within two and-a-half games back. The next day, the Dodgers dumped a doubleheader to these same Braves while the Giants were topping Philadelphia 5-1 to stunningly set the difference at one mere game.

What occurred on September 26 would not on the surface appear to alter the race, as both the Giants and Dodgers won to keep the margin at one game. But in Brooklyn's 15-5 slaughter of Boston, Robinson stole home in the eighth inning for a meaningless run with a 12-3 lead, which the Braves felt humiliated them in front of their hometown fans.

Normally mild-mannered Braves manager Tommy Holmes angrily reacted after "We were badly beaten and they needed that run like a hole in the head. All I know is that it made my guys mad and they're really gunning for them now. So they wanted to show us up? Well maybe we can fix their wagon for good." Holmes vowed " . . . They're gonna pay for it."

That next day in the final game of the Brooklyn-Boston series, the idle Giants listened nervously to the radio as Holmes' team delivered on its promise. The Braves scored the winning run in the 4-3 game on an extremely controversial play at home plate when umpire Frank Dascoli called Bob Addis safe. A rhubarb ensued, with Campanella and Roe ejected, but the standings now showed a minuscule half-game separating Brooklyn from New York.

The Giants had a rare second straight day without a game scheduled on the 28th but still managed to accomplish what almost no one in the past couple months had given them any chance of doing. In Philadelphia that day, the Dodgers had a 3-0 lead after five innings. But when Willie Jones hit a single to drive in Richie Ashburn with the winning run in the 4-3 game, New York was now a co-holder of first place in the National League. With identical records of 94-58, each team had two games remaining on its schedule—the Giants with two games in Boston, and Brooklyn with two in Philadelphia.

On that last Saturday in September, Sal Maglie would be opposed by lefty Warren Spahn, each shooting for a league-leading 23rd victory. Mays started off the scoring in the second inning when he walked, stole second and third, and scored on Don Mueller's single. That would be all they needed, though they scored two more, as Maglie got his win with a five-hit shutout. Down in Philly, Newcombe threw a shutout of his own for his 20th victory in the 5-0 win.

The last chance to settle the N.L. pennant within the confines of the standard 154-game schedule came down to Sunday, September 30. Adding more drama to an already highly dramatic situation, both games turned out to be nerve-wracking affairs ultimately settled by one run. Giants starter Jansen allowed one run on two hits in the opening frame then managed to hold the Braves hitless until the ninth inning. Thomson got New York on the board with a solo homer in the second, and another run scored on a base hit the next inning. In the fifth, the Giants got what would be their third and final run of the game when Irvin singled in Dark.

The Braves rallied in the ninth, pushing across one run and had the tying and winning runs on base with two outs. Jansen, still on the hill, was facing outfielder Willard Marshall, who had spent his first five seasons in the majors with the Giants. Marshall lofted a fly ball that landed in Irvin's glove to clinch at least a tie, keeping the miracle alive. The team had simply refused to quit despite seemingly hopeless odds, and it was Durocher who deserved much of the credit, constantly reminding them: "You never can tell."

The focus now shifted to the Dodgers-Phillies game, which not only was still in progress, but would become a marathon. The Phillies had captured the 1950 pennant by beating Brooklyn, with whom they were tied going into the final day of the season. One year later they had a good chance to knock the Dodgers out of the pennant race again.

Roe, Brooklyn's ace with 22 wins started the game on short rest and was reached for four runs in the second and was yanked. By the end of the third it was 6-1 in favor of the Phillies, and they added two more runs in the fifth. The Dodgers however, chipped away with one in the fourth, three in the fifth, and three in the eighth to tie the score at eight. This was the way it would remain for a good long time as the game went deep into extra innings.

In the bottom of the 12th with Newcombe now pitching, pitcher Robin Roberts, another starter on in relief, walked to open the inning. Later in the inning with two outs and Roberts on third with the potential winning run, first baseman Eddie Waitkus hit a hard liner toward right field that looked like it could be the game-winner. Jackie Robinson dove quickly and snared the drive, and though he came crashing down hard on his shoulder, he miraculously hung on to the ball to save the game.

The 13th passed without a run, but in the top of the 14th, Robinson further added to his heroics. With Roberts still in the game pitching his seventh inning of relief, Jackie hit a solo home run that he called the greatest hit of his entire career. In the bottom of the 14th, Waitkus, who nearly won it two innings earlier, flied to Pafko in left to ensure that an N.L. playoff series would in fact occur.

The Giants had been listening to the game on the radio in the dressing room, but had to board their train in Boston when it was in the 12th inning. They didn't learn of the results until they reached Providence Station at 6:15 p.m. When they arrived later on at Grand Central Station, thousands were on hand to cheer them. Likewise, a large crowd was at Penn Station to greet and support the Dodgers that evening.

Analysts were hailing the lineup changes and adjustments the Giants had made during the season that contributed to their miraculous finish. The four significant moves, in chronological order were: putting Whitey Lockman at first base and Monte Irvin back in the outfield; promoting Mays from the minors and immediately inserting him in the starting lineup on May 25; Adding Al Corwin to the pitching staff in mid-July as he proceeded to win four straight games; and moving Bobby Thomson to third base on July 20.

Thomson had been booed heartily by the Polo Grounds crowd on July 15 when he entered the game as a replacement for Don Mueller, but days later began to get them back in his corner. His roommate Lockman had recently encouraged him to alter his batting stance a bit, and from the time of the switch to third through to the end of the season, he hit .357, which raised his average from .227 to .293. In all, for Durocher, it may well have been the finest managerial job he would do in a career that ultimately incorporated 24 seasons.

For the Dodgers, it is only natural to wonder how they could have allowed a 13-game lead to evaporate over a seven-week span. Joe King wrote in late September:

> "The Dodgers simply stopped playing their best when they imagined they had the deal in hand, and when they let the fire die under the boilers, they found it difficult to raise steam again."

It is tempting to locate individual games or incidents that may have swung the balance in the Dodgers' favor by just that one mere game it would have taken to accomplish what most everyone believed was a foregone conclusion. Perhaps extreme ungraciousness in victory on a few occasions by Dressen and a small group of players prompted the hand of fate to reach out and deliver a slap. After the Dodgers had swept New York in the Fourth of July doubleheader, Dressen said, "They're through. Those two beatings we gave them knocked them out of it. They'll never bother us again." Dressen openly admitted that summer his personal philosophy of not wanting to let sleeping dogs lie, and in this case, it clearly came back to bite him.

There was also an incident on August 9 after Brooklyn had just completed a three-game sweep over New York in Brooklyn. They were celebrating loudly enough after the game to be heard clearly in the Giants' locker room right next door. Among the taunting remarks directed towards the visitors clubhouse was "Eat your heart out, Leo. So that's your kind of team?" as well as a song that featured the lyrics "Roll out the barrells . . . we've got the Giants on the run!"

The Giants knew that the main voices belonged to Robinson, Reese, Newcombe, and Furillo, and quite likely Dressen was not far away, smiling like a Cheshire cat. Right then and there, Durocher vowed to a reporter that there would be no further lineup changes and that he was sticking with his team to the end, which was very inspirational to his players.

Perhaps the Dodger downfall was 'the curse of Bruce Edwards,' backup catcher shipped to Chicago in the Pafko trade who came back to beat his ex-teammates in his first game with the Cubs the next day; or Dressen quoted in a late-season article in *Baseball Digest* saying the acquisition of Pafko was the move that clinched the pennant; or Gene Hermanski, another principle of that trade who predicted on that first day with his new team that the Dodgers would lose the pennant; or Hank Edwards, traded away in mid-season and later failing in an opportunity to add another loss to the Giants record; or backup catcher Rube Walker, filling in for Campanella

when he had been struck in the head in September and contributing next to nothing; Robinson, firing up a Braves team in late September with a meaningless steal of home that may have given Boston extra incentive to beat Brooklyn the next day. As always in an
extremely tight pennant race over a long season, second-guessing
and 'what-ifs' are inevitable.

Now the only thing that was inevitable was that the two National League teams that called New York home were to face each
other on Monday afternoon, October 1, to begin a rare best-of-
three playoff series. For only the second time in the league's history,
a short series was required, this time to determine who would gain
the privilege of advancing to face the New York Yankees in the
1951 Fall Classic. The Dodgers, as it would happen, were participants in the first playoff, which occurred just five years before. The
results were less than memorable for the franchise and its faithful
followers, as the St. Louis Cardinals swept their "Bums" in two games.

As the playoff got underway at the cozy ballpark on Bedford
Avenue in the borough of Brooklyn, it warranted front-page stories
not only in New York newspapers, but in many papers across the
country. The atmosphere surrounding the event was similar to that
of a World Series, yet it was still technically considered the regular
season. Game One was officially Game number 155 for both the
Dodgers and Giants, who had won a coin toss and opted to play
Game Two and Three, if there was one, at the Polo Grounds.

Neither team had either of its top two pitchers available, with
16-9 Jim Hearn facing off against Ralph Branca. With a record of
13-11, Branca had split his time between starting and bullpen work.

Pafko put Brooklyn on the board first by hitting a solo home
run in the bottom of the second inning. Two innings later, Thomson
hit a two-run shot to make it a 2-1 game. This was not the first
home run Thomson hit off Branca in 1951, and of course it would
not be the last.

The score remained the same until the eighth inning when
Monte Irvin connected for a solo home run off Branca. He was
relieved to start the ninth by Bud Podbielan, but the scoring was
complete at 3-1, with all runs coming on home runs. Except for the

one mistake to Pafko, Hearn allowed only four other hits, none for extra bases in his outstanding complete-game win. For the first time, the Giants were in sole possession of first place in the National League.

Game Two switched to the antiquated and historic Polo Grounds, located at 8th Ave. and 157th St. in Harlem, just on the fringes of Manhattan. This game was quite a contrast from the day before, particularly for Brooklyn batters. They plated two in the first as Robinson homered off Sheldon Jones, who was later replaced in the third by George Spencer. He did not fare better, nor did his replacement Al Corwin, as the Dodgers also got home runs from Gil Hodges, Pafko, and backup catcher Walker, replacing the injured Campanella. The Giant defense did not help their cause, committing five errors, and Durocher was also second-guessed for not starting Maglie.

Rookie pitcher Clem Labine pitched marvelously, allowing Giant batters just six safeties in the 10-0 drubbing. Tied once again, it all came down to a one-game season.

October 3, 1951.

To those with a fair degree of knowledge of the long history of baseball, few dates stand out as more noteworthy than 10/3/51. It would provide the game and its followers with a highlight captured on celluloid to be relived for as long as the sport shall survive.

In the stands at the Polo Grounds was the widow of the legendary manager John McGraw, a link to a considerable amount of Giant glory from the earlier part of the century. A New York victory on this overcast fall day would catapult the team to its 13th World Series appearance.

Each team was now able to send one of its star hurlers to the mound, with Maglie opposing Newcombe. The Dodgers scored one in the first on a Robinson single, and the game stayed that way until the Giants gained it back with an RBI double by Thomson in the seventh. In the top of the eighth with Maglie still in, Reese and Snider led off with singles. Maglie then shocked everyone when he threw a wild pitch that scored Reese, and both Pafko and Billy Cox followed with RBI singles to make it a 4-1 game.

Newcombe mowed the Giants down with relative ease in the bottom of the eighth, striking out the side and causing a feeling of dejection in the home team's dugout. To paraphrase the classic baseball poem "Casey at the Bat":

The outlook wasn't brilliant for
the Giant nine this day.
The score stood 4 to 1 with
but one inning to play.

Jansen came on in relief of Maglie to start the ninth and set Brooklyn down in order. Those rooting for the Dodgers were breathing a bit easier and anticipating jubilation just moments away.

Al Dark was the leadoff hitter in the bottom of the ninth and delivered a single. An untimely incident then occurred that may have caused the superstitious to wonder if Brooklyn had been jinxed, and that fate had been tempted on their behalf. A public address announcement was made informing the Brooklyn beat writers that they could pick up their press credentials for the World Series Yankee Stadium opener at the Biltmore Hotel.

Mueller, a lefty batter, was able to take advantage of Hodges holding Dark on first and drove a single through the hole as most of the 34,320 in attendance began to buzz.

The huge right hander Newcombe was laboring, but then induced Irvin to hit a pop foul to Hodges for out number one. Dressen came out to speak to Newcombe briefly, but left him in. Lockman then doubled to drive in Dark to make it 4-2 with runners on second and third. Mueller had severely sprained his ankle sliding into third on the play, and was taken off the field after being down for several minutes. Backup outfielder Clint Hartung was brought in to run for him.

At this time, Dressen had Game One starter Branca along with Carl Erskine warming up in the bullpen under the watchful eye of coach Clyde Sukeforth. With Newcombe in a jam, Dressen had called the bullpen and asked his coach which of the two appeared to be throwing better, and was told that Branca was. During the long delay with Mueller down, the Dodger manager went out to make the change. Newcombe had pitched on both September 29 and 30, and was working this game on just two days' rest. He had told Dressen during the seventh inning that his arm was tired, and in the ninth, he just felt he could not continue. Newcombe said, "This is too important a game to take a chance on my arm."

Dressen then relied upon Sukeforth's judgement and summoned Branca to face Thomson and hopefully record the final two outs of the game. Durocher, who had routinely coached third base, walked down the base line to speak to Thomson while Branca was warming up.

Many weeks later, Durocher revealed the nature of his discussion with Thomson, as well as a somewhat bizarre occurrence. He said that with about a week left to go in the season he received a letter from a fan who identified himself as "McDougald McPherson McTavish." Amazingly, the fan had predicted the outcome of the last several games of the season correctly, and even stated that Thomson would win the pennant with a home run.

Durocher claimed that he had only told a few of the players about the letter, and said that when he walked over to talk to Thomson, he pulled the letter out of his pocket to show him. Leo then urged, "If you ever hit one, hit one now." Durocher would later question why Brooklyn didn't walk Thomson to get to Mays, who had been slumping. Thomson had already hit several home runs off Branca in '51.

Thomson stepped in, and Branca's first pitch was a fastball that umpire Lou Jorda called a strike. Then at 3:57 p.m., Branca, who wore uniform No. 13, and had 13 victories that season, let go the unluckiest pitch of his life. It seemed to have nothing on it, crossing the heart of the plate as Thomson took full advantage. He drove the ball on a line, and it just cleared the fence in left as Pafko stood at the base of the wall helplessly. As Thomson circled the bases, soldiers a half a world away were able to share in the moment as the international broadcast prompted it to be dubbed "the shot heard 'round the world." On a local level, it capped off what was just as affectionately known as "the Miracle of Coogan's Bluff." As he arrived at home plate, Thomson was mauled by his teammates and carried off the field to the clubhouse in center field. Again, paraphrasing "Casey":

BOBBY THOMSON. *Of the 264 major league home runs that Bobby Thomson hit over his 15-year career, it was this home run swing that cemented his place in baseball history.*

For there is no joy in
Brooklyn . . . mighty Thomson . . .
. . . hit one out.

Thousands of fans spilled from the stands and marched out to the clubhouse door and chanted for Thomson and his teammates to appear for curtain calls. For the Glasgow-born Thomson, who was occasionally referred to as "The Flying Scot," it was an absolute storybook moment. In the city, tickertape fell from office building windows, fans danced in the streets, and a spontaneous parade began in Times Square. To this point in the long history of the game, Thomson's home run was almost without question its most dramatic and significant ever struck.

As for the unfortunate individual who delivered the fateful pitch, Branca would forever be known as the goat in this historic

RALPH BRANCA. *Signed by the Dodgers off the sandlots of Brooklyn, Branca would be somewhat unfairly regarded as one of the biggest goats in the history of the game.*

LEO DUROCHER AND BOBBY THOMSON. *A locker room celebration of the most famous and historic incident from baseball in 1951.*

game. This would be the case despite having won 21 games as a 21 year old in 1947, or contributing to three National League championship teams. Branca was sobbing almost uncontrollably in the clubhouse after the game, wondering why such a fate should befall him. Years later, he said, "I accepted that it would be something I would have to bear for the rest of my life."

But nearly 50 full years after the famous incident, information came to light that may have eased Branca's burden somewhat. It appears that the Giants may have employed tactics along the way in their pursuit of the pennant that were less than scrupulous.

These tactics became public knowledge upon the publication of an article by Joshua Harris Prager in the January 31, 2001 edition of the *Wall St. Journal*. Citing sources such as Monte Irvin, Bobby Thomson, and Sal Yvars, it was revealed that on or around July 20, a telescope was set up at the Polo Grounds in a clubhouse window in deep center field in order to read the opposing catcher's signs. A buzzer system was set up in the Giants bullpen, where the sign was then relayed to the batter. The Giants reportedly continued this skulduggery for the balance of the season at the Polo Grounds, but Thomson maintained that he did not know what pitch was coming when he connected for his famous home run.

The story caused considerable furor among baseball historians. Researcher David W. Smith, a member of the Society of American Baseball Research pointed out shortly after that the Giants' batting average, on-base percentage, and slugging percentage was actually slightly lower at home after July 20 than it had been before. Another member, Christine Fry reminded fellow historians of what Bill Veeck had revealed in his 1962 biography *Veeck—As in Wreck*. He stated that his 1948 A.L. Champion Indians had employed similar tactics down the stretch and ultimately won the pennant in a one-game playoff. It was also known to many that legendary manager John McGraw had utilized various sign-stealing systems during his career.

It is important to note that although the practice was clearly unethical, there technically was no written rule forbidding it until 1961. In all likelihood, such methods were employed at various times throughout baseball history.

The Giants had now completed what surely seemed an impossible mission seven weeks prior. Including the three-game playoff that had just abruptly concluded, they had won 39 of their last 47 games for a stunning .830 winning percentage over that span. Yet there was barely enough time to savor the accomplishment as the A.L. champion Yankees had been waiting three days to engage in the World Series that would open less than 24 hours away.

In light of what had just occurred, even a World Series would seem almost anticlimactic.

BOBBY THOMSON'S *bat and cap that he used when he hit his famous home run, on permanent display at the Baseball Hall of Fame. Courtesy: National Baseball Hall of Fame.*

15

YANKS ROAD TO "THREE-PEAT"

AS SPRING TRAINING OF 1951 WAS WIND-
ING DOWN, there were many question marks and causes for
concern in the Yankee camp that could conceivably interfere with a
quest in which the only acceptable conclusion was yet another A.L.
pennant.

It was unclear how many games Joe DiMaggio might be able
to play with the nagging injuries he was experiencing, and when he
did play, would he perform up to his lofty expectations? Young
Mickey Mantle, slated to play beside him, would be sticking with
the team, but making the jump from Class C ball was a giant step.

Another untested youngster making a big jump to the Yankee starting lineup was infielder Gil McDougald, who was making
a big impression on Stengel in spring games. He would likely be
filling a void left by Bobby Brown, who was serving an internship as
a doctor in San Francisco.

Stengel was concerned over a lack of depth with the loss of Brown, as well as the retirement of longtime right fielder Tommy Henrich, now acting as a Yankee coach. The pitching staff would be operating without young lefty Whitey Ford, who had come up as a rookie in 1950 and won his first nine decisions. Ford had traded in his Yankee pinstripes for Army uniform. Heading into the '51 campaign rookie right hander Tom Morgan was being elevated from Class B Binghamton to hopefully pick up the slack. Despite so many factors that might plant a seed of doubt, Stengel let it be known in late March that he was sure the Yankees would win their third straight pennant.

Stengel's image as a rather comical character, with his almost Professor Irwin Corey-like ramblings was disputed at this time by Franklin Lewis of the *Cleveland News*:

> "He wins because he masquerades a native shrewdness about baseball with a clown's approach. He kids his players. He mocks them on the bench. Yet they think he's still a funny man, a fine ribber."

With Opening Day fast approaching, the Yankees had health issues with a few key players. Allie Reynolds had an inflamed right elbow and had yet to pitch in the spring; southpaw reliever Joe Page had an inflamed pitching shoulder; and Phil Rizzuto had pulled a muscle on his left side. All three flew to Johns Hopkins Hospital in Baltimore to be examined in mid-April. The Yanks' woes were not lost on the sportswriters across the league, as most picked them to finish second behind Boston. Even Joe DiMaggio thought the Red Sox would be tougher than ever, in part due to the addition of Lou Boudreau.

The team got a break when Brown was able to return to the team on April 24, and Billy Martin's Army discharge put him back in a Yankee uniform a day later. Twenty-year-old Morgan pitched well a few days later on April 28 against Washington at Yankee Stadium and got his first major league win. Mantle was establishing

CASEY STENGEL. *Though many feel that Stengel was fortunate to be managing a team such as the Yankees, he performed a masterful job in taking them to their third straight pennant.*

himself, at least for the time being, as the starting right fielder, and McDougald was showing his versatility and value by switching back and forth from third base to second base as needed.

Gil had a game for the ages just two-and-a-half weeks into his rookie season on May 3 in St. Louis when he drove in six runs in one inning. In his first at-bat in the ninth inning he hammered a two-run triple, and later in the same inning with a Yankee rally still in progress, McDougald came up again and slugged a grand slam. The Yanks set a record with 11 runs in the ninth inning in the 17-3 slaughter. Equally important, Reynolds was able to pitch his first game of the year and got the complete-game win.

The White Sox offered the stiffest competition early in the season, pulling out in front in May. From May 4 to June 6, Chicago won 25 of the 29 games they played in a streak that was being called "the Miracle on 35th St." The span included a 14-game winning streak that was finally snapped on June 2. The Yanks met the first-place White Sox in Chicago for a four-game series beginning on June 8, a game that saw a record crowd of 53,940 at Comiskey Park. New York took the first three games, but Chicago averted the sweep by winning the final, and clung to a two-game lead.

Stengel revealed three days later on June 13 that Yogi Berra had hit safely in eight of his last nine games, remarkably, with a cracked bat. Included in the span was an upper-deck home run. Berra became known throughout his career as a notorious bad-ball hitter, but perhaps at times such as this, he was also a bad-bat hitter.

In mid-June, Yanks G.M. Weiss made a serious bid to acquire Browns ace Ned Garver. New York fans were disappointed when they were unsuccessful and instead had to settle for the addition of reliever Stubby Overmire from the Browns in exchange for long-time Yankee lefty Tommy Byrne.

The White Sox maintained their hold on first place from May 28 until early July, when Boston took over for nearly two weeks. The Yankees had been as close as one-half game out on July 1, but didn't do themselves any favors by dropping a Fourth of July doubleheader to Washington, then getting swept in a three-game series in Boston going into the All-Star break. The White Sox were struggling far worse, as from June 15 up to the midway point they were a mediocre 13-15, and their hold on first place was about to come to an end for good.

DiMaggio was for the most part a non-factor in the month of July, and Mantle had been skidding badly enough to warrant his demotion to the minors by mid-month, but Yankee starting pitching was more than pulling its weight. Still pitching despite bone chips in his right elbow, Reynolds had a scoreless streak that was finally snapped at 32 1/3 innings on July 2. The same inning that streak ended, his 37 2/3 straight innings of not allowing a walk also came to an end. Ten days later, the spotlight shined brightly on him when he opened the second half of the season by no-hitting the Indians at Cleveland.

Lefty Eddie Lopat, on the way to leading the team in ERA and co-leading in wins was the staff's representative at the All-Star Game. On July 29, Vic Raschi became the second A.L. pitcher after Bob Feller to reach the 15-win plateau. Ted Williams was quoted in an Oscar Ruhl column of July 18 saying, "Vic Raschi is the best pitcher alive. There just can't be anyone else as good. I admire that guy."

Raschi actually pitched throughout the season with floating cartilage, which he would have removed after the season. He revealed that it did not allow him to run between starts in order to stay in top condition. Even spot starter Morgan had moments of brilliance—none more so than his 1-0 complete game shutout over Garver and the Browns on July 20. As the season went on, Morgan was occasionally referred to as "the (Whitey) Ford of '51."

It was on that morning of July 20 that only five percentage points separated the top four teams. It was Boston at .598; Chicago, .596; New York, .595; and Cleveland, .593.

Two days later, on the strength of a sweep of a doubleheader over the Browns in St. Louis, the Yankees were on top by a mere two percentage points over both Boston and Cleveland. On July 24, New York was to begin a three-game set against the rival Tribe at Yankee Stadium. The Yankees prevailed in the first two contests by the narrow margins of 3-2 and 2-1, and only Feller was able to prevent a sweep by winning the final game 9-4.

As the calendar turned to August, the standings showed that the Yankees at 59-35 still occupied the top spot with a two-game bulge over Cleveland. It soon became clear that it was the Indians, with their marvelous starting pitching, that would stand in the way of the New York pennant hopes. The favored Red Sox suffered a variety of woes that prevented them from living up to expectations. 1950 Rookie of the Year Walt Dropo had broken his wrist in Spring Training, and when he returned his timing was off, and he was sent to the minors in June. Lou Boudreau broke his hand and missed almost half the season. Slugging infielder Vern Stephens was hampered by a leg injury and was limited to 90 games in the field. Bobby Doerr had severe back problems and played only six games after August 7.

New additions to the pitching staff, Ray Scarborough and Bill Wight both had ERAs above 5.00. The Red Sox pitching staff had fewer complete games than any team in the league, with 46.

Throughout the month of August, it was New York and Cleveland battling for the top spot. By the time the two were scheduled to meet for a three-game series in Cleveland on the 23rd, the Indians had pulled into the lead by a modest two games. Two days before, Feller had become the first A.L. pitcher in '51 to win 20 games. Bob Lemon had the Yanks' number in the opener, holding them to just one run on three hits as Cleveland increased their lead to three. New York came back the next day with a combined 2-0 shutout from the unlikely duo of Overmire and Joe Ostrowski in a game that saw the return of Mantle from the minors. The next day, Mantle homered and doubled as the Yanks copped the finale to pull within one game of the lead. The race had captured the interest of the Cleveland fans, as a total of 160,531 attended the three games.

On August 29, the Yankees made a transaction that they felt would give the pitching staff a boost for the stretch run. That Wednesday at 4 p.m., they announced that they had acquired longtime Braves right hander Johnny Sain in exchange for minor league pitcher Lew Burdette and $50,000. Many teams subsequently complained about the waiver rule that allowed the Yanks to obtain a proven hurler of Sain's caliber. As the rule was written, only N.L.

teams had to waive on him in order for the Braves to be able to deal him to the A.L. team of their choice. The waiver price was only $10,000, so the financially strapped Boston team very likely convinced other N.L. teams not to claim him so that they could sell him to an A.L. team for much more money. Remarkably, Sain was offered to the Red Sox, but general manager Joe Cronin asked for more time, then called back later to say he couldn't use him because he had no room on the roster. Sain pitched a complete-game five-hitter in his first game with New York on September 3, beating Philadelphia 3-1.

The Yankees had been one game up on Cleveland heading into September, and the schedule seemed to favor them. New York would be playing 20 of their remaining games at Yankee Stadium, while Cleveland had only eight games left at home. The two would go head to head for the final time in a brief two-game stint on September 16 and 17 in the Bronx. Going in, Cleveland led by just percentage points as Feller was matched up against Reynolds in a Sunday game that saw the Stadium's biggest crowd of the year at over 68,000. Feller didn't survive the fifth, and Reynolds completed the 5-1 win for his 15th win of the season. New York's winning percentage of .624 now topped Cleveland's .621, a lead they would not relinquish. They previously had sole possession of first place seven times this season, but this time it was for keeps.

The next day Lopat out-dueled Lemon 2-1 for his twentieth victory. The teams remained close until Cleveland traveled to Detroit to begin a three-game series and were subsequently swept, then lost their next game in Chicago. Ultimately, the Indians failed because they lacked balance. Pitching was their main asset, and when it failed near the very end, they fell out of the race. They were the first A.L. team in 20 years with three 20-game winners in Feller, Wynn, and Garcia, but their team batting average was next to last in the league; they committed the most errors; and only Washington turned fewer double plays.

New York had the chance to clinch against Philadelphia on September 26, but Bobby Shantz prevented it by tossing a six-hit shutout on his 26th birthday. The celebration had to wait two days until the Yankees swept a doubleheader from Boston on the 28th. The opener was Reynolds' second no-hitter, and the second win, which was the actual clincher, was Raschi's 21st victory. The general belief among the New York press that Stengel would resign if the Yankees didn't win was now a moot point as they were headed for their 18th World Series in the past 31 seasons.

Athletics manager Jimmie Dykes, praising Stengel for the job he did, said that this edition was the worst of all Yankee teams, and "old time Yankee heroes must shudder" watching them. He noted, however, that they had the ability to win the big game, the one that simply must be won, while other teams did not possess this ability. "Perhaps it is tradition. Perhaps it is fine organization. Maybe it is the Yankee uniform. I don't know exactly. Perhaps more likely, it is a combination of all these factors." Washington columnist Shirley Povich called winning the '51 pennant Stengel's "greatest triumph."

He referred to DiMaggio being too far over the hill; not having a reliable winner after Reynolds, Raschi, and Lopat; and Rizzuto and Mize getting old and tired. Indeed, day after day it seemed, Stengel had to shuffle his lineup and batting order, playing hunches all the while.

The Yanks did possess a fairly well-balanced attack, yet there were no truly outstanding offensive performances. With the exception of McDougald at .306, no regular hit .300, and Berra, who led with 88 RBI, was the only Yankee to crack the 20-homer plateau. Lopat and Raschi led the pitching staff with 21 wins apiece, and Reynolds, with 17, certainly had his share of fine performances. His team-leading seven shutouts led a staff whose combined total of 24 shutouts was an impressive 13 more than Chicago, the next-highest team. To top it all off, the Yankees had the support of the fans, who topped the majors by filling the Stadium to the tune of 1,950,107.

As those fans filed out of the Bronx ballpark on Sunday afternoon, September 30 at the conclusion of Game number 154, they would have a three-day wait to find out which of their inter-city rivals they would hopefully be reigning triumphant over in the upcoming Fall Classic.

16

'51 FALL CLASSIC IN REVIEW

WHILE THE TERM "SUBWAY SERIES" has become virtually a household phrase, some were referring to the Yankees-Giants matchup of '51 as the "Rowboat Series." The teams' ballparks were situated a mere three-quarters of a mile apart, nestled on the opposite banks of the Harlem River. With the all-New York City locale, many of the big local banks were able to procure tremendous blocks of tickets for executives and clients, leaving many of the loyal, working-class fans left out. As a result, the Series was also bitterly referred to as a "mink-clad, Park Avenue affair monopolized by big shots," Even the New York football Giants were displaced, having to move their October 7 game versus the Detroit Lions from the Polo Grounds to Detroit.

With the N.L. playoff just concluded the day before, Yankee Stadium was the site of the opening game on Thursday, October 4. Most of the writers seemed to favor the Yankees to win, partly due to the notion that any further competition may seem anti-climactic to the Giants in light of the manner in which they had just dispatched their archrival Dodgers. Also because of the just-concluded playoff, the Giants were unable to open with one of their top starters, sending 10-9 Dave Koslo in Game One. Stengel had the luxury of setting his rotation as he saw fit, with Reynolds, Lopat, and Raschi, in that order.

Among the dignitaries on hand for the occasion were former president Herbert Hoover, General Douglas MacArthur, Heavyweight boxing champ Jersey Joe Walcott, and FBI head J. Edgar Hoover. Lucy Monroe sang the National Anthem, accompanied by Guy Lombardo's Royal Canadians. Newly-elected commissioner Ford Frick handled the task of tossing out the ceremonial first pitch for the first time in his new capacity as 65,673 looked on.

With the action underway, Reynolds retired the first two batters he faced, Eddie Stanky and Al Dark. He then issued a walk to Hank Thompson, who was seeing his first action of the year in the outfield, filling in for Don Mueller, who injured his ankle the day before. A Monte Irvin single and a Whitey Lockman ground-rule double brought home Thompson to open the scoring. Irvin then immediately pulled off an exciting steal of home with playoff hero Bobby Thomson at bat to give the Giants a quick 2-0 lead. It was the first steal of home in World Series play in 30 years.

The score remained the same until the bottom of the second, when with one out, Gil McDougald stroked a double off Koslo into the left field corner. Jerry Coleman then came up and singled to right, and when Thompson, who was normally a third baseman, bobbled the ball, McDougald was able to score. The game then remained tight with a 2-1 score until the top of the sixth when the Giants proceeded to make a bit more noise.

With two outs and runners on first and second, Dark pulled a home run into the left-field stands, which for all practical purposes put the game out of reach. Koslo, born George Bernard Koslowski had shut the door on the favored Yankees. The pitcher, who had been with the Giants longer than any member of the team allowed just the one tally and scattered seven hits in the complete game 5-1 win.

Irvin had an outstanding day, going 4-for-5 with a triple and three singles. He would have had a fifth hit if his scorching liner wasn't nabbed at first base by Joe Collins. Irvin also made the fielding play of the game in the first when he robbed Hank Bauer of a game-tying home run.

The Giants had not experienced a letdown as some expected, and managed to go one up in enemy territory.

The teams went right back at it the next day, as Eddie Lopat was matched against Larry Jansen. Just having completed his fifth major league season, Jansen was now regarded as one of the finer pitchers in the league with two 20-win seasons and an overall record of 96-57.

After an uneventful top of the first, Mantle, bunting on his own, laid one down just past the mound and was safe at first. Rizzuto followed with another bunt between the mound and first base, and when Whitey Lockman fielded it, he threw wildly to first.

With runners now on first and third, McDougald singled to right, bringing across Mantle to put the Yanks on the board first. First baseman Collins added a solo home run with two outs in the second inning to increase the lead to 2-0. From that point through the end of the sixth inning, the only hit by either team was a harmless single by Dark in the top of the sixth. The only noteworthy occurrence during the middle portion of the game was the seemingly serious knee injury to Mantle in the fifth at which time he was carried off on a stretcher. He was replaced in right field by Bauer.

The Giants finally got into the scoring column in the top of the seventh. They opened the inning with singles from Irvin and Lockman, and Irvin later scored on a sacrifice fly from pinch hitter Bill Rigney. The Giants had a chance to tack on more, but Ray Noble, pinch hitting for Jansen, fouled out to Berra with two on to end the threat. The score now stood at 2-1.

Bobby Brown became the first Yankee baserunner since the second inning when he led off the bottom of the eighth with a single to center off George Spencer. He was immediately pinch run for by Billy Martin, and a few batters later, Lopat helped his own cause by driving in Martin with a single for an insurance run. This would close out the scoring as Lopat pitched a fine five-hit game, going the distance in the 3-1 win. The A.L. champs had evened the Series up at one, and they would now move across the river to the ancient Polo Grounds for the next three games.

The following day, October 6, the Giants reached back into their history in the opening ceremonies as Mrs. John McGraw tossed out the first ball. The all-time great pilot's widow had watched her late husband take his team to ten World Series, and had seen the glory days from Christy Mathewson to Bill Terry. The 53,035 in attendance was the largest crowd to ever attend a World Series in an N.L. park, and most of the younger fans were pleased to see Perry Como sing the Anthem.

Jim Hearn was opposed on the hill by "The Springfield Rifle" Vic Raschi, who had won 21 games for the third year in a row. It was Hearn however, who had the better stuff on this day. He did allow singles to Rizzuto and McDougald in the opening frame, but got DiMaggio to fly out to end the inning with no damage. After a harmless slow roller that Berra beat out to open the second, Hearn did not give up another hit until the eighth inning. The Giants got on the board in the bottom of the second when Thomson led off the inning with a double down the left field line, and young Mays got his first Series hit and RBI as he singled to right to score him. The score would remain 1-0 in favor of the Giants until the bottom of the fifth.

After Hearn struck out to start the inning, Raschi walked Stanky. Then came a play that touched off a minor controversy involving the pesky Giant second baseman. With the hit and run sign on, Dark missed the pitch, but when Berra threw down to Rizzuto covering, Stanky kicked the ball out of his glove and into center field as he was sliding.

This was a stunt that Stanky was known to pull now and then, and after he got up and scampered to third the Yankees complained fruitlessly. Dark then singled to make the score 2-0. Thompson singled, sending Dark to third, and when Irvin bounced to third, he threw home but Berra dropped the ball and allowed him to score. Whitey Lockman came up and proceeded to hit a three-run homer into the lower right-field stands, chasing Raschi from the game. The Yankees got a rally going in the eighth, and when Hearn walked Collins with the bases loaded and two out, the Giants brought in Sheldon Jones.

Bauer bounced back to Jones to end the inning, and the only other scoring was a Gene Woodling solo homer in the ninth as the 6-2 win put the Giants up 2-1.

Two hours after the game, a reporter heard the following exchange between Dark and Stanky after almost everyone else had left:

> *Dark:* "Gee, I hate to go home. I just wish I could sleep here so that I could be up and after them so much earlier in the morning. It's the waiting for game-time that I hate."
>
> *Stanky:* "You and me both. If I had my way, I'd never leave here during a series like this one."

Durocher had acquired both Dark and Stanky from the Braves in December of 1949 with owner Stoneham's approval and really believed that they were his kind of ballplayers. He would not be disappointed, and both would go on to noteworthy managerial careers themselves.

Game Four was scheduled for the next day, Sunday, October 7, but rain forced its cancellation. The Series resumed on Monday, with Reynolds going against Maglie, making his first World Series appearance.

The Giants got on the scoreboard first in the bottom of the first when Dark doubled off the left-field wall and was brought home two batters later on an Irvin single. The Yankees would come right back in the top of the second as Woodling doubled down the left-field line. McDougald then grounded to third, but Thomson bobbled it to give the A.L. champs two on with none out. A couple batters later, Collins singled in Woodling to tie it at one.

The Yankees added an RBI single in the fifth, and DiMaggio connected for his final series homer, a two-run shot in the fifth to make it 4-1. Cold weather may have affected Maglie, as he just couldn't get loose. He gave way to Sheldon Jones to start the sixth, and he was reached for two unearned runs in the seventh to give the Yankees a commanding 6-1 lead.

The Giants started a rally in the ninth, and Thomson drove in Hank Thompson with a single. With only one out and runners on first and third, Mays came up, but grounded into his third double play of the game to end it.

Veteran writer Fred Lieb wrote that the Sunday rainout may have been a turning point for the Yankees and gave Reynolds another day of rest. Reynolds did manage to complete the game, but was constantly in trouble. He had a count of three and two on ten batters, but when he needed to get one over he came in with a good, hard, effective fastball.

The following day, October 9, was to be the final game of the Series held at the Polo Grounds. Young singer Eddie Fisher, who was a Private in the Army at the time delivered his rendition of the Star Spangled Banner before the game. The pitching matchup was a repeat of Game Two, with Jansen trying to avenge his loss to Lopat on that day. It started off well enough for the Giants, as Dark singled in the first then came around to score on an Irvin single and a Woodling error. In the end however, that would stand as the lone highlight of their game.

In the third, the Yanks exploded for five runs, four of which came on McDougald's grand slam. He was the first rookie to ever connect for a slam in series play. The next inning, with Jansen out of the game and lefty Monte Kennedy in, Rizzuto was attempting a hit-and-run and was surprised when he hit the ball into the right field stands for a home run. It was said to be the first opposite-field homer he had ever hit in the majors. It was 7-1 after the fourth, and though it was over for the Giants, it was far from over for the Yanks. They rallied for two in the sixth, and four more in the seventh as many of the Polo Grounds crowd had long since departed. When the carnage was over, the home team had suffered a 13-1 beating.

Lopat had pitched his second complete game five-hitter, and compiled an ERA of 0.50 for the Series.

When Durocher was asked afterwards what he thought the turning point was, he replied, "When they played the National Anthem. We didn't have a chance after that."

Now with a 3-2 lead, the teams headed back to Yankee Stadium for Game Six on October 10. Vic Raschi would try to clinch it for the Yankees, while Dave Koslo was trying to extend it to a seventh game. Before the game, Ralph Branca visited the Giants clubhouse to wish them good luck, then went out and graciously posed for photographs with Bobby Thomson. Each team would score its first run on a sacrifice fly—McDougald driving in Coleman in the first, and Stanky bringing home Mays in the fifth. Going into the bottom of the sixth it was still 1-1, but the Yanks were about to do damage.

A Berra single, an intentional pass to Joe D., and another walk to Johnny Mize loaded the bases. Bauer, who had done virtually nothing thus far in the Series came up and ripped a triple to deep left field to make the score 4-1.

The Giants came back the next inning and opened with singles by Mays and pinch hitter Rigney. Stengel then went to the bullpen and brought in Johnny Sain, who got the Yanks out of a potential jam by retiring by retiring the next three batters to end the inning.

Durocher's men tried to get a rally going in the eighth after the first two batters were set down. Thompson walked, Westrum singled, and Mays walked to load the bases. Again Sain worked out of a jam when he struck out pinch hitter Ray Noble to retire the side.

With Jansen now on to pitch the bottom of the eighth, DiMaggio doubled to lead off in what would be his last major league at-bat. They failed to score, however, and the game would move on to the ninth with the Yankees still holding a 4-1 lead. But the Giants were not about to go quietly.

With Sain still on the mound, they opened the inning with a single by Stanky, a bunt down the third base line that Dark beat out, and a Lockman single to shallow center to load the bases.

DiMaggio scooped it up and threw it in, touching a ball for the last time in his fabulous career.

Sain would not be allowed to work himself out of this one, as Bob Kuzava was brought in to pitch. The first two batters he faced, Irvin and Thomson, both hit sacrifice flies to left that now made it a mere one-run game at 4-3.

With Lockman still on second base, Durocher sent up backup catcher and New York City native Sal Yvars to pinch hit for Thompson. Yvars had hit a pinch hit home run to win a game for the Giants in June. This time he connected with a low line drive that looked as though it was going to drop in to tie the game. Bauer raced over and managed to snare it just six inches off the ground. He had lost the ball in the late afternoon shadows and wasn't even sure he had it until he looked in his glove. The Yankees could now raise the World Championship Banner for the 14th time in their history.

As for the Giants, Durocher admitted after their weak bench had hurt them in the Series. But he did add: "All I know is that they never quit. They went down battling to the last out. They didn't win, but they're still champions in my book—all 25 of them."

It had been a truly amazing year for the city that three major league teams called home. In light of the N.L. playoff, the all-New York World Series, and the subsequent election of the MVPs coming from the local teams, Dan Daniel would call it the biggest year in New York baseball since the Knickerbockers drew up the first set of rules.

MCMLI: AN HISTORIC BASEBALL TIME AND PLACE

17

WHEN 2001 BASEBALL HALL OF FAME inductee Dave Winfield was born on October 3, 1951, it would forever be considered only the second most significant baseball occurrence on that day. New York Giants third baseman Bobby Thomson and his bat, which is on permanent display in Cooperstown, provided baseball with the absolute defining moment for the calendar year of 1951. No recollection of classic baseball moments would ever be complete without a reference to the Thomson home run and all that surrounded it. Reviewing the particulars, the incident appears to include all of the elements that make for a legendary moment for the ages that in some ways seems to grow over time rather than diminish.

The factors of time, place, and circumstance seem to have blended together with beautiful precision. The nostalgic feeling that is invariably attached to the 1950s; the site of the classic Polo Grounds where so much baseball history took place; and hallowed and beloved figures such as Jackie Robinson, Gil Hodges, Willie Mays, and others competing in a game that would send one team on to face the mighty Joe DiMaggio-led New York Yankees in the World Series, while the other team would go home in defeat.

There are some who may point out that Thomson's legendary home run did not help the Giants win the 1951 World Series, and in a sense it may have gone for naught. Yet can anyone conclusively state that had he not hit it, the Brooklyn Dodgers also would not have gone on to beat the Yankees? A different conclusion in the fabled playoff game may well have changed the course of baseball history.

When an industry such as Organized baseball produces a highlight so prominent and lasting as the Thomson home run in the course of a season, the by-product is that many other noteworthy performances and achievements become overshadowed or overlooked entirely. With players such as Ted Williams, Stan Musial, Ralph Kiner, Bob Feller, and Warren Spahn all still operating in the prime of their careers, their exploits on the playing field warranted considerable attention and admiration from the press and fans alike.

Williams was attempting to return from a broken elbow suffered in 1950, and doctors had feared the injury might seriously curtail his continuing as one of the game's great hitters. By mid-'51, the Boston surgeons were very surprised by the progress of Ted's comeback. Red Sox trainer Jack Fadden, who helped devise a therapy regimen said of Ted's rehab, "This guy has more energy than you'll possibly believe. He never stopped working. We had to slow him down. All he ever thought about was getting that elbow strong again."

In mid-May, Williams was surprisingly criticized by no less than Ty Cobb on his hitting style. Cobb said:

> "Williams has fine ability, but no player can be called a truly great hitter unless he can hit the ball to all fields. Ruth could choke up his bat and hit to left field any time he wanted. He had everything necessary to earn his place among the baseball immortals."

Williams was stung by the criticism after reading the quotes in the newspaper, and proceeded to let his bat respond. On May 21 against Cobb's old Detroit team, he had three hits that were all to the opposite field—a single, double, and home run that helped win the game for Boston 9-7. Williams received a big compliment from White Sox pitcher Joe Dobson, a longtime former teammate of his who said in July "He's got great eyes, but he's got two other things that make him the hitter he is: the ability to check his swing if a breaking ball crosses him up, and the freedom to hit any time, even on a 3-0 pitch."

Ted still had his battles with certain reporters, as his distaste for them collectively has been well-documented. When he first encountered writer Lou Miller of the *New York World-Telegram and Sun* in July of 1951, he said to him "So you're a baseball writer? You're no good—until you prove otherwise." A couple of weeks later, *The Sporting News* quoted Ted as saying, "Not all baseball writers are bad. I know a few good ones. But if I had my way, none of them would be allowed in any clubhouse."

Ted also had a few biting words in February when writer Jimmy Burns asked what he thought of *Sporting News* Editor J.G. Taylor Spink's suggestion that there should be a $35,000 limit on player salaries. "I think Mr. Spink is full of prunes. A man is worth all he can get. That holds true in any line of work, and you may rest assured that no employer is going to pay a man more than he's worth. In fact, it's hard to get it."

Ted actually had for him what may have been a very slightly below average season individually in '51, yet he still hit .318 with 30 homers and 126 RBIs. Many didn't realize that his performance may have been affected by playing the second half of the season on a bad knee. His manager Steve O'Neill said after the season that it likely cost him numerous hits. One major milestone he did achieve was becoming the 11th player in history to reach his 300th home run, which came on May 14 at Fenway Park against Chicago's Howie Judson. Other milestone home runs reached in '51 by noteworthy sluggers were Stan Musial's 200th, and Gil Hodges' 100th. As for

Musial, he also captured the fifth of his eventual total of seven N.L. batting titles this season, which would ultimately leave him only one shy of Honus Wagner's league record of eight. Wagner himself would be spending his final season in '51 suiting up as a coach for the Pirates at their home games.

At the conclusion of the '51 campaign, Musial's lifetime batting average of .3473 was now tops among active players, surpassing Ted's .3466. In June, Williams had said that Musial was the only hitter he knew who unloaded all of his power into every swing and still maintained a high average. Jackie Robinson also gave Stan high praise, saying after the season: "Musial is the greatest all-around player in the game today." In early October, *The Sporting News* named him the Outstanding Player in the N.L. in '51.

While Musial was clearly the circuit's top hitter, Pirates star Ralph Kiner was once again its premier slugger, winning the league home run crown for an unprecedented sixth consecutive season. His career home run pace of one every 12.6 at-bats was the best among all active players by a wide margin. On July 18, Kiner hit three home runs at Ebbets Field and flied to deep center field in the ninth, narrowly missing a fourth. He said after that he swung for the fences deliberately only a few times in his career, but that was one of those times. Two days later, July 20, the Babe Ruth Foundation announced the establishment of the "Babe Ruth Home Run Award," which would go to the leading home run hitter in the majors each year. The trophy would be displayed in the Babe Ruth room at the Hall of Fame, and not surprisingly, Kiner would be its recipient in '51 and '52, the first two years of its existence.

The Pirates had experimented with Kiner at first base at the beginning of the '51 season rather than left field, but abandoned the move after 58 games. Though he much preferred the outfield, Kiner was reluctant to switch back because he was concerned that fans would believe he was asking out due to the pressure of learning a new position. A few weeks after the season ended, Kiner explained, "I lost lots of weight, and I think it hurt my home run hitting. And I realize I'm no cat around that bag, so I think it hurts the team's chances too." If Kiner's statement was accurate, one might wonder if his 42 home runs could have reached 50 had he spent the entire season in his familiar left field position.

George Kell, the Tigers exceptional third baseman had another outstanding season in 1951. The former batting champ managed to lead the A.L. in hits, was a co-leader in doubles, and ranked third in the loop in the batting race. In a game against St. Louis on May 13, Kell hit safely an incredible six times. The All-Star third sacker also stood out defensively, leading in assists, double plays, total chances per game, and fielding percentage.

The Philadelphia Athletics, despite their mediocre 70-win sixth-place finish, dominated the batting triple crown categories. Outfielder Gus Zernial led the league in both home runs with 33, and RBIs with 129. On May 17, he tied a record by hitting his seventh home run in the previous four games. First baseman Ferris Fain captured the batting title with a .344 mark, becoming the first Athletic to do so since Jimmie Foxx in 1933. Fain barely qualified for the title due to missing 37 games because of a rather freak injury. On July 15, after an unsuccessful at-bat, he kicked the first base bag and broke his foot in four places. He returned to the lineup on August 21, and manager Jimmie Dykes subsequently moved him up to second in the batting order so that he would get more at-bats, but made him promise not to kick anything.

There were several prominent pitching performances during 1951, with Preacher Roe's 22-3 record establishing a record for winning percentage. Warren Spahn, who wore uniform No. 21, had won 21 games three times already in his five full seasons going into 1951, and went on to reach that figure a total of eight times in his career. The Braves lefty won his 21st of '51 on September 16 with a five-hitter over the Reds, but still had a few chances left to add to the figure. Spahn then chose a novel, albeit superstitious method in order to attempt to attain win No. 22. Just before the September 25 game versus Brooklyn, Warren borrowed teammate George Estock's number 22 jersey and wore it as he beat the Dodgers that day in a 6-3 complete game. Hoping for further success with this formula, Spahn borrowed Johnny Logan's No. 23 on the next-to-last day of the season against the Giants. The Braves were unable to score any runs for him that day as he left after eight innings down 2-0, finishing up the season at 22-14.

Very early in the season on April 23, Spahn's 29th birthday, he performed a pitching feat that seems remarkable decades later. He worked all 16 innings of a 2-1 loss to the host Dodgers, losing when third baseman Gene Mauch booted a ball with two out that led to the winning run.

Such ironman feats on the mound were not entirely unusual back in a time when a starter was expected to finish a game. At least two other similar situations were witnessed in the Summer of '51. On July 12, Saul Rogovin of the White Sox pitched all 17 innings in a loss to the Red Sox. Incredibly, he came back five days later to beat the Yankees in a ten-inning complete game. Around the beginning of the 21st century, there would be many starting pitchers who might not compile that many total innings in five consecutive starts.

And the day after Rogovin's 17-inning marathon, Mickey McDermott of the Red Sox pitched 17 innings of his own in a 19-inning game.

Of all the newsworthy items in baseball in 1951, there were, of course, many that were of a less positive nature. Several managerial changes occurred throughout the year, beginning with the resignation of the Braves' Billy Southworth on June 19. Southworth had achieved success with the Cardinals earlier, taking them to the World Series three straight years from '42 through '44. He had also skippered the Braves to the Series against Cleveland in '48, losing in six games. Southworth had been distressed by the Braves' continued losses in early '51, and when they were shut out by the Cubs on June 19, he made his decision public. It was speculated that Southworth knew that he was about to be fired and opted to resign first.

The Braves then hired Tommy Holmes, who was managing their Hartford affiliate in the Eastern League at the time. An outstanding outfielder for the Braves previously, he had retired after the '50 season to take over Hartford but would now be coming back as a player-manager. Holmes took over and won his first game as manager, which prompted Leo Durocher to say, "After that win in his first start, (he) should resign as manager of the Braves. He will never be any happier than he is tonight." Indeed, Holmes' tenure with the financially troubled, mediocre team would not be a terribly rewarding experience.

A little over a month later on July 21, the Cubs dismissed Frankie Frisch after a 5-0 loss to the Phillies. The manager, who had 16 years' experience as a big-league pilot seemed to now be constantly getting thrown out of games, which did not go over well with his bosses. Still, Wid Mathews, Cubs director of player personnel assured everyone a week before the firing that Frisch was safe and that no change was being contemplated. A few days later, several players criticized their manager anonymously, of which management took note, and it did not help that the team was floundering in seventh place.

Frisch was a taskmaster in the mold of one of his early mentors John McGraw, and he even imposed 25 dollar fines if he saw his players fraternizing with members of the opposing team. Frisch was now the first member of the Baseball Hall of Fame to be fired from a major league managerial job after he had already been enshrined in the institution. He was replaced by Cubs first baseman Phil Cavaretta, who would also remain active as a player.

The ax fell on three other managers shortly after the season ended. The Browns did not retain Zack Taylor, which was a foregone conclusion, as Rogers Hornsby was hired as the new manager on October 8. A couple of weeks later, on October 22, Lou Boudreau was hired to replace Steve O'Neill as manager of the Red Sox. One of the conditions he insisted upon from Sox owner Tom Yawkey when he was offered the job was the power to trade anyone on the team, to which the owner reportedly agreed.

Very shortly after, Boudreau began to hint that Ted Williams could be available in the right deal. One former Red Sox player said in November, "If Boudreau can make an advantageous deal for Ted Williams, his temperamental left fielder, he would be doing himself and the club a considerable favor." Williams and Boudreau were clearly not friendly. Williams resented Boudreau, regarding him as one who undermined his domination of the team, while Boudreau seemed to feel that Ted stifled enthusiasm on the team. Boston writer Bob Ajemian wrote in late November " . . .Williams is definitely headed to another American League club."

Several potential trades were reportedly discussed involving Ted in the month of November. A deal with Washington involving Eddie Yost was mentioned. Boudreau considered a Williams for Chico Carrasquel swap with the White Sox, but Chicago G.M. Frank Lane said he wouldn't consider it. He added " . . . no proper price can possibly include our All-Star Game shortstop, especially in a deal for a 33-year-old outfielder who couldn't play shortstop with the aid of three arms and a lacrosse racquet."

On November 12 at a luncheon in Chicago, Boudreau said he wouldn't trade Ted for Ned Garver, and when Bill Veeck later heard about it, indicated that he wouldn't make the deal either. Veeck questioned, "Who would give up a 20-game winner, a .305 hitter by the way, for an outfielder who hit .318 and has never distinguished himself defensively?" A Joe D.-for-Ted trade was discussed briefly, and the Indians were also interested, but would only part with one starting pitcher.

In early December, Boudreau did an about-face on trading Williams and announced at baseball's Winter Meetings in New York on the 8th that he was taking him off the trading block. Perhaps he was disappointed at the lack of good offers for Ted, but he now said he would not consider any deal.

A half-century later with the legendary, almost god-like status Ted Williams has risen to within the world of sports, it is difficult to imagine teams refusing to extend themselves to acquire his services. To look in retrospect at the career of a Chico Carrasquel, and to learn that the White Sox would not sacrifice him for a player of Williams' stature seems utterly remarkable.

There was still one more managerial transaction that would occur before the end of 1951. Cardinals owner Fred Saigh was not pleased when manager Marty Marion asked for a two-year contract after a distant third-place finish and an improvement of only three wins over the previous season. He also took note of the fact that

Marion had been signed as a player-manager for '51, yet didn't play at all. When Marion chose to go hunting rather than attend the Winter Meetings, Saigh had seen enough, and traded for the Giants' Eddie Stanky and named him player-manager. In the end, of the five managers who lost their jobs in 1951, only Marion would ever manage a major league team again.

Aside from the front-page news story of DiMaggio's retirement in December, a few other noteworthy players saw their major league careers come to a close. Terrific Red Sox second baseman Bobby Doerr suffered a severe back injury on August 7 and one month later played what would be his last game. On September 22 before a Red Sox-Yankees game, the man who had played more games in a Red Sox uniform up to that time than any other player stepped up to the microphone to say goodbye to the fans at Fenway Park. At the age of 33 he would be going home to Eugene, Oregon, to tend to his farm.

One highlight Doerr experienced in '51 was to have reached his 2000th hit, which he got at the expense of Eddie Lopat on July 1. At the time, the only active players to have reached that figure were Joe DiMaggio and Wally Moses. By year's end, all three would have joined the ranks of the retired as Moses ended his fine career to accept a coaching position with the Athletics. Wally took with him the distinction of having hit over .300 his first seven seasons. And Johnny Vander Meer, back-to-back no-hit artist and three-time strikeout leader pitched his final game, coming with the Indians on May 7.

Aside from the drawn-out situation that culminated in the naming of a new commissioner, one other significant off-field story involved the major congressional investigation on the business of baseball. The House Committee on Study of Monopoly Power, an 11-member panel that was a branch of the Judiciary Committee would be conducting the probe. Representative Emanuel Celler (D., N.Y.), the chairman of the committee announced in late May that hearings would begin in the summer, and had been prompted by lawsuits against Organized baseball and bills that were filed to exempt the game from anti-trust legislation. The panel would be seeking definitive answers to two major questions: Was Major League Baseball a business or a sport?, and was the reserve clause necessary in the operation of baseball?

The hearings would consist of two one-to-two week sessions, the first of which would begin on July 30. It delved mainly into the Reserve Clause; territorial issues, which also included television and radio broadcast rights; the possibility of expansion; and the Pacific Coast League's desire to become a major league. Among the well-known baseball figures who were called to testify were Ty Cobb, who led off, Ford Frick, Happy Chandler, and National Association president George Trautman. Most who testified at the first session agreed that the Reserve Clause was necessary to the smooth operation of the game. New York State Representative Kenneth Keating was highly critical of the hearings at this time. He said, "Congress better be darned careful before it starts tampering with baseball. From the start I've been lukewarm about conducting an investigation. At a time when the world is on fire, it seems to me that we have more important things to do."

Much of the public seemed to wonder why Congress was investigating baseball, which was thought to be the cleanest sport there was. A common sentiment was that if any sport should be probed, it should be boxing.

The second session resumed on October 15, and focused primarily on the draft process, waiver rules, player limits, salary minimums, and arbitration. These hearings featured witnesses such as Larry MacPhail, team owners Clark Griffith and Phil Wrigley, Will Harridge, Branch Rickey, J.G. Taylor Spink, and even active players Pee Wee Reese and Lou Boudreau. The second session concluded on October 24, and the committee declared that decisions should be forthcoming within a few months.

In the end, nearly a half million words of testimony were spoken, yet ultimately no significant changes were mandated in the operation of baseball. In addition, all lawsuits by players challenging the Reserve Clause were dismissed by year's end.

Baseball managed in 1951 to make its presence felt in movie theaters, bookstores, and even retail stores where bubble gum cards were sold. "Angels in the Outfield," a baseball fantasy that premiered in theaters in September starred Paul Douglas as manager of the Pirates. The movie included cameos of major leaguers and scenes shot at Forbes Field, the Polo Grounds, and Sportsman's Park. Two other baseball movies released in '51 included "Rhubarb" starring Ray Milland, and "On Moonlight Bay". Hollywood studios had also begun filming movies on the lives of Dizzy Dean and Grover Cleveland Alexander in late '51, though they would not be released until the following year.

Late April saw the publication of Thompson and Turkin's *Official Encyclopedia of Baseball*, a 640-page reference book that was nearly 20 years in the making. It was hailed as the most comprehensive work ever published on the game, as it was the first significant attempt at a statistical documentation of its history.

And Topps Bubble Gum cards, which would become a part of so many childhoods for decades to come made their debut in the Spring of '51.

So many various aspects of the game existed at that time that have now long faded from its landscape. Not only were the Negro Leagues still operating, the All-American Girls Professional Baseball League continued to maintain a 112-game schedule in outposts such as Rockford, Illinois, South Bend, and Fort Wayne, Indiana, as well as five other Midwestern cities. The longtime favorite 'House of David' touring team also still criss-crossed the country entertaining fans.

There were serious murmurings that change lay ahead for baseball, and in fact the 1950s would bring about unprecedented changes for the game. Many agreed that the West Coast was ready for major league ball. No one would have possibly drawn a connection when Dan Daniel predicted in his column in October that before another decade, city housing would replace the Polo Grounds; or when Walter O'Malley called Ebbets Field "obsolete" in August, and said, "We need a new park. But where to place it?"

Baseball teams, ballplayers, and the game itself may have lost a lot of its hallowed, almost sacred status in society over the many decades, but it still held such a lofty position in America in 1951 that Yankees owner Del Webb was moved to say this in April of that year:

> "Baseball is one of the greatest things these United States could possibly have. The nation would not die if we did not play ball. But try to picture the U.S.A. minus baseball."

And former U.S. president Herbert Hoover had stated later in November that baseball ranks next to religion in its influence for good in the United States.

Indeed, that was baseball a half-century ago.

Appendix A

1951 FINAL STANDINGS AND LEAGUE LEADERS

American League

	Won	Lost	PCT.	G.B.
New York	98	56	.636	-
Cleveland	93	61	.604	45
Boston	87	67	.565	11
Chicago	81	73	.526	17
Detroit	73	81	.474	25
Philadelphia	70	84	.455	28
Washington	62	92	.403	36
St. Louis	52	102	.338	46

National League

	Won	Lost	PCT.	G.B.
New York	98	59	.624	-
Brooklyn	97	60	.618	1
St. Louis	81	73	.526	15 1/2
Boston	76	78	.494	20 1/2
Philadelphia	73	81	.474	23 1/2

Cincinnati	68	86	.442	28 1/2
Pittsburgh	64	90	.416	32 1/2
Chicago	62	92	.403	34 1/2

LEAGUE LEADERS

American League - Batting

Batting Average

Ferris Fain	Phila.	.344
Minnie Minoso	Cleve., Chi.	.326
Ted Williams	Bos.	.319

Hits

George Kell	Det.	191
Nellie Fox	Chi.	189
Dom DiMaggio	Bos.	189
Minnie Minoso	Cleve., Chi.	173

Doubles

Sam Mele	Wash.	36
Eddie Yost	Wash.	36
George Kell	Det.	36

Triples

Minnie Minoso	Cleve., Chi.	14
Ray Coleman	St. Louis, Chi.	12
Nellie Fox	Chi.	12
Bobby Young	St. Louis	9

Home Runs

Gus Zernial	Chi., Phila.	33
Ted Williams	Bos.	30
Eddie Robinson	Chi.	29

Runs Batted In

Gus Zernial	Chi., Phila.	129
Ted Williams	Bos.	126
Eddie Robinson	Chi.	117

Runs scored

Dom DiMaggio	Bos.	113
Minnie Minoso	Cleve., Chi.	112
Ted Williams	Bos.	109
Eddie Yost	Wash.	109

Stolen Bases

Minnie Minoso	Chi.	31
Jim Busby	Chi.	26
Phil Rizzuto	N.Y.	18

American League - Pitching

Wins

Bob Feller	Cleve.	22
Ed Lopat	N.Y.	21
Vic Raschi	N.Y.	21
Ned Garver	St. Louis	20
Mike Garcia	Cleve.	20
Early Wynn	Cleve.	20

Earned Run Average

Saul Rogovin	Det., Chi.	2.78
Ed Lopat	N.Y.	2.91
Early Wynn	Cleve.	3.02

Strikeouts

Vic Raschi	N.Y.	164
Early Wynn	Cleve.	133
Bob Lemon	Cleve.	132

Shutouts

Allie Reynolds	N.Y.	7
Ed Lopat	N.Y.	5
Bobby Shantz	Phila.	4
Bob Feller	Cleve.	4
Vic Raschi	N.Y.	4

Winning Percentage

Bob Feller	Cleve.	.733
Ed Lopat	N.Y.	.700
Allie Reynolds	N.Y.	.680

National League - Batting

Batting Average

Stan Musial	St. Louis	.355
Richie Asburn	Phila.	.344
Jackie Robinson	Brook.	.338

Hits

Richie Ashburn	Phila.	221
Stan Musial	St. Louis	205
Carl Furillo	Brook.	197

Doubles

Alvin Dark	N.Y.	41
Ted Kluszewski	Cin.	35
Roy Campanella	Brook.	33
Jackie Robinson	Brook.	33

Home Runs

Ralph Kiner	Pitt.	42
Gil Hodges	Brook.	40
Roy Campanella	Brook.	33

Runs Batted In

Monte Irvin	N.Y	121
Ralph Kiner	Pitt.	109
Sid Gordon	Bos.	109
Roy Campanella	Brook.	108
Stan Musial	St. Louis	108

Runs Scored

Ralph Kiner	Pitt.	124
Stan Musial	St. Louis	124
Gil Hodges	Brook.	118

Stolen Bases

Sam Jethroe	Bos.	35
Richie Ashburn	Phila.	29
Jackie Robinson	Brook.	25

National League - Pitching

Wins

Larry Jansen	N.Y.	23
Sal Maglie	N.Y.	23
Preacher Roe	Brook.	22
Warren Spahn	Bos.	22
Robin Roberts	Phila.	21

Earned Run Average

Chet Nichols	Bos.	2.88
Sal Maglie	N.Y.	2.93
Warren Spahn	Bos.	2.98

Strikeouts

Don Newcombe	Brook.	164
Warren Spahn	Bos.	164
Sal Maglie	N.Y.	146
Larry Jansen	N.Y.	145

Shutouts

Warren Spahn	Bos.	7
Robin Roberts	Phila.	6
Ken Raffensberger	Cin.	5

Winning Percentage

Preacher Roe	Brook.	.880
Sal Maglie	N.Y.	.793
Don Newcombe	Brook.	.690

Appendix B

1951 SALARIES OF SELECTED MAJOR LEAGUE PLAYERS BASED ON REPORTS IN VARIOUS PUBLICATIONS

Ted Williams	$125,000
Joe DiMaggio	$100,000
Stan Musial	$75,000
Ralph Kiner	$65,000
Bob Feller	$50,000
Phil Rizzuto	$50,000
Lou Boudreau	$40,000
George Kell	$40,000
Hal Newhouser	$38,000
Jackie Robinson	$36,000
Andy Pafko	$35,000
Hoot Evers	$34,500
Yogi Berra	$30,000
Pee Wee Reese	$30,000
Larry Doby	$28,000
Enos Slaughter	$27,000
Del Ennis	$25,000
Billy Goodman	$25,000
Robin Roberts	$25,000
Vic Wertz	$25,000

Jim Konstanty	$22,500
Birdie Tebbetts	$22,000
Charlie Keller	$20,000
Sal Maglie	$20,000
Roy Campanella	$19,000
Whitey Lockman	$18,000
Ned Garver	$18,000
Don Newcombe	$17,500
Jim Hearn	$16,000
Eddie Yost	$16,000
Walt Dropo	$15,000
Luke Easter	$15,000
Granny Hamner	$15,000
Sam Jethroe	$15,000
Jack Kramer	$15,000
Virgil Trucks	$15,000
Billy Cox	$14,000
Dan Bankhead	$12,000
Monte Irvin	$12,000
Hank Thompson	$12,000
Mickey Mantle	$7,500
Willie Mays	$5,000

Appendix C

MISCELLANEOUS ITEMS FROM 1951

- Ten years after his brother Joe's famous consecutive-game hitting streak, Dom DiMaggio had a 27-game hitting streak of his own that ended in June.

- Yankees catcher Clint Courtney became the first major league catcher to wear glasses in a game in May of 1951.

- Future president Ronald Reagan performed play-by-play broadcast duties along with Harry Caray for the St. Louis Cardinals game on 6/20/51 vs. the Giants

- Chuck Connors, later known to television audiences as "The Rifleman" was starring at first base in 1951 for the Los Angeles Angels of the Pacific Coast League, and also appeared briefly with the Chicago Cubs.

- The 1951 American Legion National Championship team, Crenshaw Post 715 from Los Angeles featured future Hall of Famer George "Sparky" Anderson and future major league infielder Billy Consolo.

- Minor league shortstop Don Zimmer of Elmira of the Eastern League was married at home plate before a game in August.

- The St. Louis Cardinals played a doubleheader against two different teams on 9/13/51. They played the Giants in the first game, and the Braves in the second. This was the first time this occurred since 1899, and would not happen again until September of 2000.

- The 1949 A.L. Rookie of the Year Roy Sievers and the '50 A.L. Rookie of the Year Walt Dropo were both sent to the minor leagues just three days apart in June of '51.

- Phillies pitcher Karl Drews got a hit on 9/22/51, snapping a hitless streak that went back to May of 1947—a span of 77 at-bats.

- In addition to the birth of Dave Winfield, 1951 also produced future major leaguers Bert Blyleven, Goose Gossage, Dave Parker, Dwight Evans, Buddy Bell, and Bill Madlock, among the more noteworthy.

Bibliography

Books

Clark, Dick, and Lester, Larry, Editors. (1994). *The Negro Leagues Book*. Society for American Baseball Research.

Cohen, Richard and Neft, David. (1985). The Sports Encyclopedia (6th ed.). St. Martins.

Fiorito, Len, and Marazzi, Rich. (1982). *Aaron to Zuverink*. Avon books.

Golenbock, Peter. (1986). *Bums*. Pocket Books

Hageman, William. (1996). *Honus: The Life and Times of a Baseball Hero*. Sagamore Publishing.

Helyar, John. (1995). *Lords of the Realm*. Ballantine.

Holway, John. (1992). *Blackball Stars: Negro League Pioneers*. Carroll and Graf.

Honig, Donald. (1987). *The All-Star Game. The Sporting News*.

Honig, Donald. (1990). *The Boston Red Sox*. Prentice Hall Press.

Johnson, Dick, and Glenn Stout. (1995). *DiMaggio: An Illustrated Life*. Walker.

Kahn, Roger. (1973). *The Boys of Summer*. Signet Books.

Lowry, Philip. (1992). *Green Cathedrals*. Addison Wesley.

Mantle, Mickey, with Gluck, Herb. (1986). *The Mick*. Jove.

Mays, Willie, with Sahadi, Lou. (1989). *Say Hey*. Pocket Books.

Okkonen, Marc. (1991). *Baseball Uniforms of the 20th Century*. Sterling.

Redmount, Robert (1998). *The Red Sox Encyclopedia*. Sports Publishing.

Reichler, Joseph. (1986). *Baseball's Greatest Moments*. Bonanza Books

Stout, Glenn, and Johnson, Richard A. (2000). *Red Sox Century* Houghton-Mifflin.

Thornley, Stew. (2000). *Land of the Giants: New York's Polo Grounds* Temple.

Ward, Geoffrey C., and Burns, Ken. (1994). *Baseball: An Illustrated History*. Knopf.

(1996). *The Baseball Encyclopedia* (10th ed.). Macmillan.

(1986). *Cooperstown: Where the Legends Live Forever*. Arlington House.

(1992). *20th Century Baseball Chronicle*. Publications International Ltd.

(1985). *Topps Baseball Cards*. Warner Books.

(1951). *1951 Baseball Official Guide. The Sporting News*.

(1952). *1952 Baseball Official Guide. The Sporting News*.

Magazines

The Sporting News
Saturday Evening Post
Newspapers
Boston Globe
Boston Herald
New York Daily News
New York Journal-American
New York Post
New York Times